Tales of the Dales

by

Ian Scott Massie

IAN SCOTT MASSIE'S artistic roots lie in the British Romantic School of the 1930s and 40s. He combines the visual style and philosophy of artists such as Paul Nash and John Piper with the palette and painterly freedom of Turner and Whistler in pursuit of the personality of the landscape. His poetic and lyrical influences have been diverse, touching on Tennyson and Hopkins, Dylan (both Bob and Thomas) and Mitchell (both Adrian and Joni).

He found his spiritual home in Masham, Wensleydale, in the late 1980s and this continues to be a major source of inspiration in a rich and energetic artistic life.

Other books include:
Under a Northern Sky
Journeys
The Paintings & Prints of John Degnan
The Penhill Giant

ISBN 978-1-909260-07-8
Published by:
Masham Gallery Press
24, Market Place, Masham, HG4 4EB

www.mashamgallery.co.uk
www.ianscottmassie.com

Tales of the Dales

The Yorkshire Dales are a rich source of stories and legends. There are families who can trace back hundreds of years their tenancy of a particular farm or house, or their ownership of one of the many estates which are scattered across the hills. This land has been settled by Celts, ruled by Vikings (who divided it into Ridings), invaded by Romans, Scots and English (it wasn't formally part of England until 955) and its villages and towns carry names in which the legacy of these various races live on. Similarly the English dialect in which these stories have been told in the past is rich with words, expressions and accents drawn from many places, particularly Scandinavia and Scotland.

The stories themselves fall into two piles. There are unique tales of individuals and places which find no echo in the rest of British folklore and there are local variations on stories which crop up in many other places which have developed heir own Yorkshire twist. Within these two groups are tiny anecdotes and the iceberg-tips of enormous stories.

I collected these tales to find inspiration for a series of paintings. The search has taken me to all parts of the Dales including some where I had never been before – quite a surprise for someone who has been exploring and painting the Dales for twenty five years. I have arranged the stories by the Dales from which they come but between Dales there are often large areas where some of the stories originate. I ask the reader's forgiveness if I have chosen to put in Swaledale something they feel belongs in Wensleydale.

Where are the Yorkshire Dales?

The Yorkshire Dales are often assumed to be the area enclosed by the Yorkshire Dales National Park, however this leaves out several bits which are also, by character, geography, geology and history, also Yorkshire Dales. Until 1974 a large part of Teesdale was in Yorkshire and therefore qualifies. Nidderdale was left out of the park because its upper reaches held a string of reservoirs and was therefore thought to be too "industrial" – a ridiculous concept to anyone looking down from Great Whernside to Scar House reservoir. Mallerstang also failed to make the cut but, hemmed in as it is by Great Boar Fell and Nine Standards Rigg its Dales' character is perfect. So in this book I have taken a generous view of what constitutes the Yorkshire Dales and therefore beautiful little Colsterdale is included, the sheep and beer market town of Masham and the headwaters and lower reaches of the great Dales rivers: the Swale, Ure and Wharfe.

One interesting bit of trivia – just to warm you up for all the other bits coming in the following text:

The Dales are centred on part of the Pennine Hills a name that came about through a bit of geographical jiggery-pokery. According to R W Mitchell in *High Dale Country,* Charles Bertram, a professor at Copenhagen University in the eighteenth century, brought to light an ancient map of Roman Britain – a forgery, as it happens – which shows the hills which form the spine of England as the *Alpes Penina*. This corruption of the Italian Appennine Hills was adopted by Conybeare and Philips when they produced their study of the rocks of Northern England as recently as 1822 and the name has stuck ever since.

This book is dedicated to the people of the Yorkshire Dales.

The Yorkshire Dales

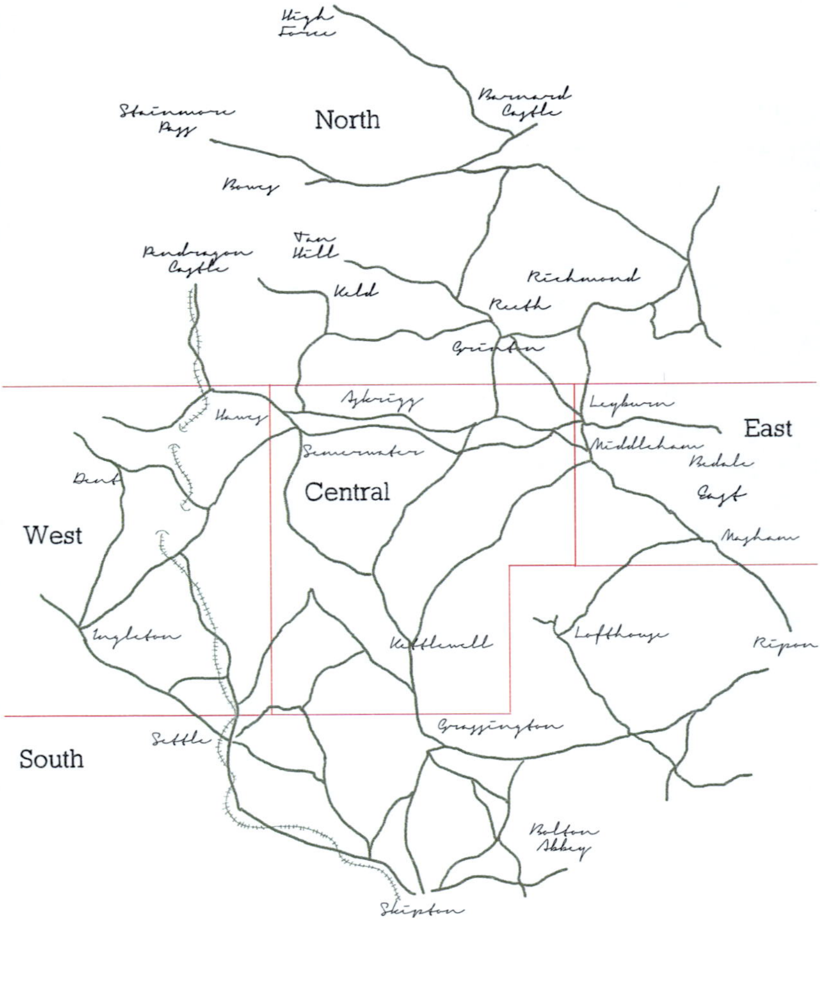

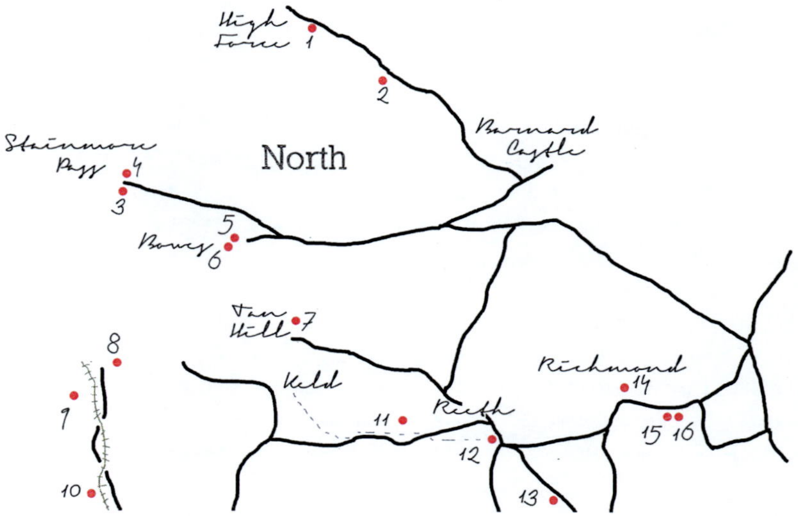

1	High Force
2	The White Houses
3	The Hand of Glory
4	Eric Bllodaxe
5	The Roman Gold of Bowes Castle
6	The Bowes Lovers
7	The Road to Tan Hill
8	Pendragon Castle
9	Wild Boar Fell
10	Hawes Junction Railway Accident
11	T'Auld Man
12	The Swaledale Corpse Way
13	James Herriot Conversion on the Road To Reeth
14	Willance's Leap
15	Potter Thompson
16	The Drummer Boy

High Force

In the upper reaches of the Tees valley Yorkshire comes to an end just above the waterfall of High Force. The main fall of High Force thunders down to the southern side of the central rock. The northern fall is frequently a trickle and sometimes disappears in dry spells. There is, however, a phenomenon known locally as The Roll when a sudden surge of water turns both falls into steaming torrents. The Roll usually happens after a period of intense rain. Further up the dale the Pennine Hills are honeycombed with caves which gradually fill with water, taking in the run-off from the fells. A point is reached, though, when the limestone levels can hold no more and, quite suddenly, the water has nowhere to go but into the Tees.

On such a day – the 24th June 1880 - two men were clambering over the rocks of High Force when, with an unmistakable rumble, the water flow increased dramatically, the river level rose and, where the northern fall had been a dry channel, there was a fast flowing waterfall. Calling to their friends a plan was drawn up. While the river level continued to rise, a rope was found and was thrown to the men. The first tied himself on firmly and was pulled through the churning water to safety. The rope was thrown a second time. The repeat of the operation began well but, whether the rope was at fault, or the weight of water too great, the rope parted and the man was swept to his death.

The visitors did not know the falls, or they might have both lived, since there is no record of the waters ever covering the central rock. It might have taken a while, but they would have survived.

High Force amazed me when I first saw it in 1974 – a black and white photo survives of a scruffy hippy in a leather jacket with a roll-up dangling from his lip – and it still amazes me. Even when the water is low the fall is impressive but see it in spate and its awesome.

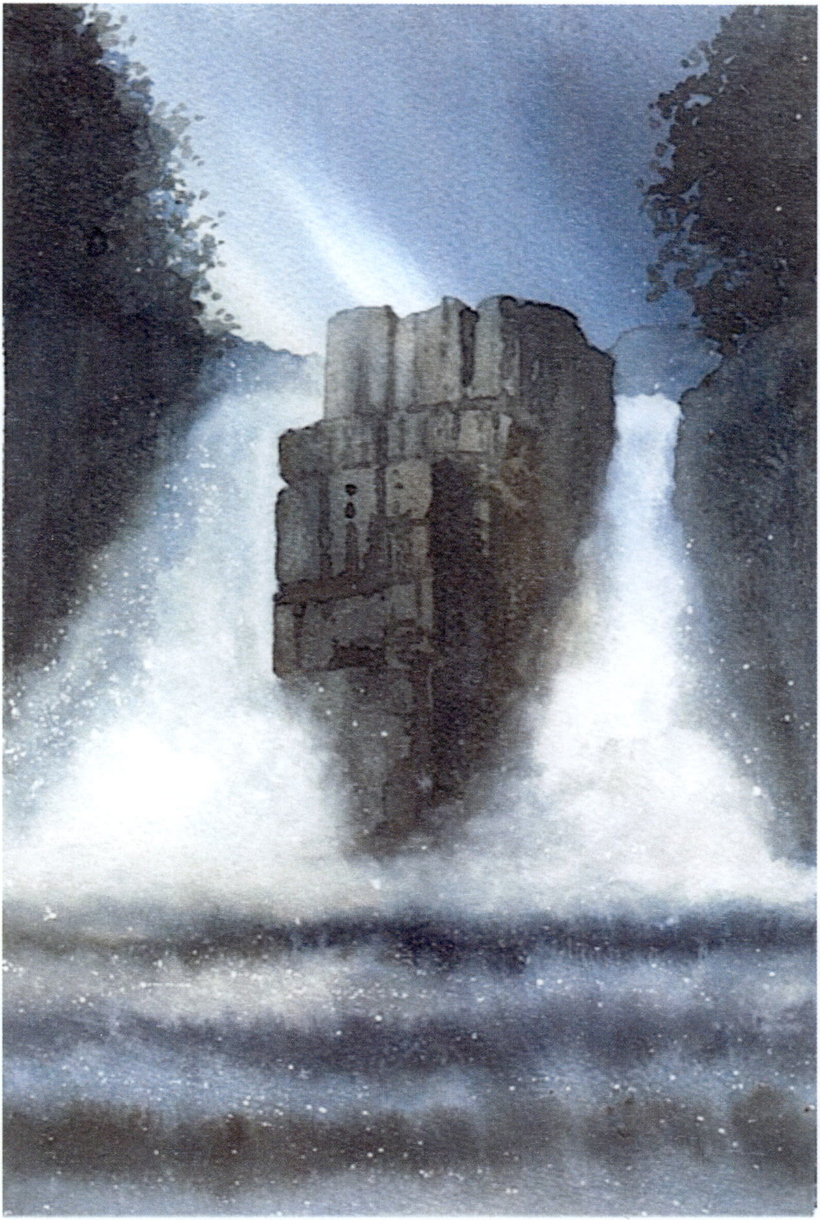
High Force

The White Houses

Scattered throughout the Dales are the estates of grand houses – the relics of the mighty holdings of Yorkshire's abbeys, castles and manors - that have been inherited, split up, parcelled out and subdivided by a whole string of monarchs, abbots, earls, industrialists and business conglomerates. On several of them there is a longstanding tradition of lime washing or white washing the houses and, on several of these, this story is told.

A brutal, bullying and basically bad medieval lord was intending to exercise his droit du seigneur – the right to take the virginity of any of his serf's daughters, prior to their marriage. He had lusted from a distance after this especially beautiful girl, had heard of her betrothal and decided to claim his immoral, but legally sound, rights. He wasn't much of a people person, so he usually made a call of this kind after imbibing a generous quantity of wine and in the company of several large, loyal men of unsympathetic disposition.

He was therefore rather drunk when, on a rainy night as black as your hat, he thumped on the farmhouse door, forced an entry and ravished the maiden he found within. As he emerged, sated, and a little shaky, his right hand man, approached him carrying a sodden parchment map and a very worried expression.

It seems that unfortunately for everyone, particularly the maiden, he had strayed off his estate, entered the home of a well-respected yeoman (who was on good terms with the local magistrate) and thereby landed himself in severe trouble.

To make sure the same mistake never recurred he had all the houses on his estate painted white – a tradition that continues to the present.

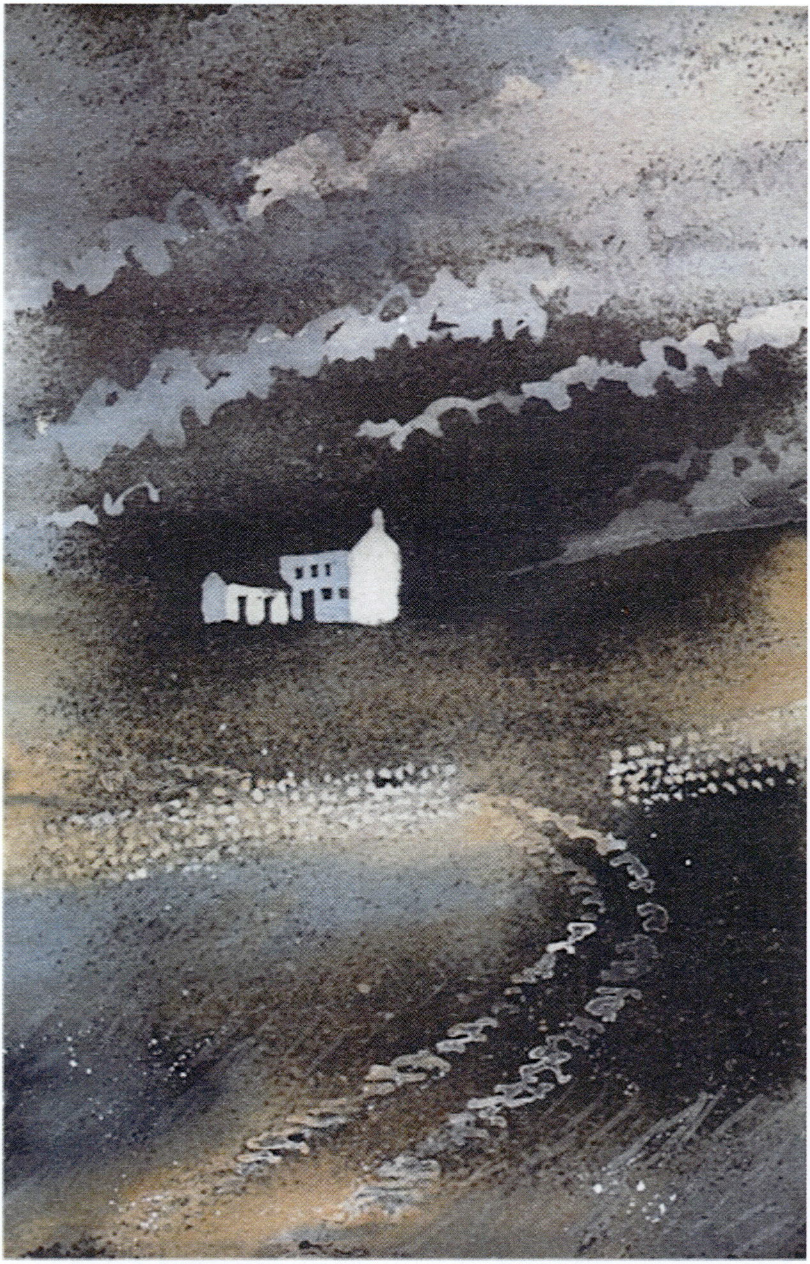

The White House, Stonesdale

The Hand of Glory

There was, an old, old house on the road sliding up toward Stainmore Pass. It was known as the Old Spital Inn and stood on the site of a 12th Century monastic hospital belonging to Marrick Priory.

One night a lady stopped to pass the night but insisted that she must leave early the next morning and that, if a little breakfast was left out for her, she need not disturb the rest of the household.

The landlord and his wife asked the maid to make sure the lady was comfortable and to lay out some breakfast before retiring, which she did but, as she was banking up the fire, she noticed a pair of trouser legs beneath the lady's skirt. All thought of sleep banished, she lay down on a couch and, after a respectable interval, settled into a rhythm of convincing snores.

The lady, who of course was nothing of the sort, took from his coat a Hand of Glory*.

**A Hand of Glory Recipe:*
Take the corpse of a man who is freshly hung from the gallows, and sever his hand at the wrist. Squeeze out as much blood as you can.
Taking some of the remaining corpse, render it down (boiling or microwaving both work well) to gather a quantity of fat.
Preserve the hand with saltpetre and season well with salt and pepper and leave in a stoneware jar for two weeks.
Place the hand in a hot oven – 230 degrees/gas mark 8 – for an hour before removing and shaping the hand to form a fist.
Take some of the rendered human fat and make a candle (scented or unscented – it seems to make no difference) that is then forced into the grip of the fist.
Your Hand of Glory is now complete and, when lit and accompanied by the right spell, will render all those asleep unwakeable.

The robber placed the Hand of Glory on the table, lit the candle made from the dead flesh and said:
"Let those who are asleep be asleep,
Let those who are awake be awake."

He then went to the door of the inn and, after drawing back the bolts, stepped out into the night and whistled to his accomplices. However it was at this moment that the maid, rising from her feigned slumber, gave the robber a hearty shove, slammed the door and pushed home the bolts.

She ran upstairs but could not wake the landlord nor any of his family as they lay locked in their enchanted sleep. Hearing the disgruntled robbers attempting o force the door, she acted on a surprisingly effective instinct and, sweeping up a bowl of milk, she doused the flame of the Hand of Glory. Instantly the sleepers awoke and, hearing the noise at the door, the landlord's son leaned out of an upper window to ask the men their business.

They replied that, if they could have the Hand of Glory, they would do no harm and be on their way. By way of reply the lad discharged a blunderbuss and, in a clatter of old iron, a cloud of smoke and a spattering of blood, the robbers took to their heels. And, in the best tradition of a traditional tale, were never seen again.

When I heard this story, from Janet Degnan of Bowes, it came with a small coda:
A storyteller had visited the village school and told the story which, of course, most of the children knew, as they also knew which house it referred to. The audience included a small girl who lived in the house in the story but her parents, thinking it might upset her, had never told her the tale. She went home, very cross, and apparently gave them a right earful!

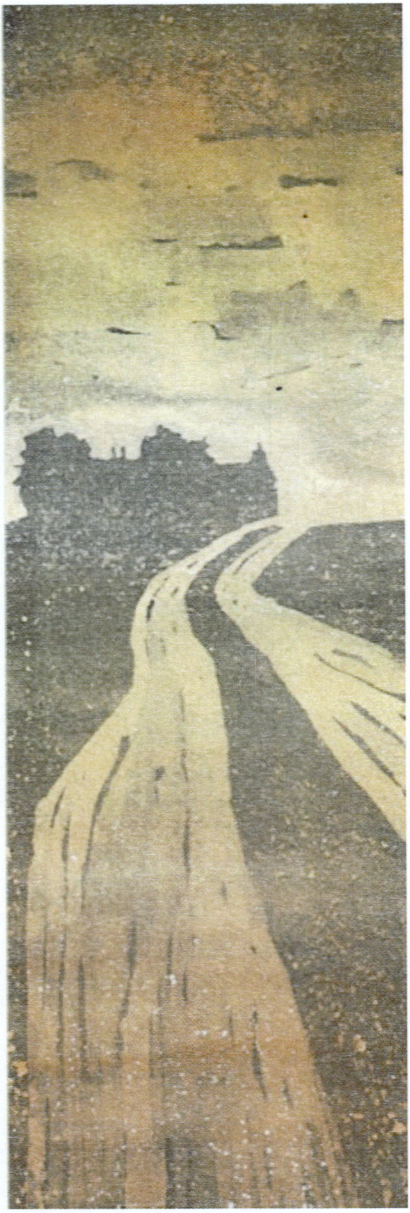

Stainmore Pass

Eric Bloodaxe

Eric (885 -954) was a Viking who waded through a sea of gore (he murdered his four older brothers who stood between him and the throne) to become King or Norway. After he was ousted as the Norwegian monarch he crossed the North Sea and established himself as King of Northumbria in the capital of York.

His reign was bitter and bloody. When the English invaded Northumbria and destroyed Ripon Minster Eric persued the fleeing army and caught them at Castleford where he made a great slaughter of his enemies.

However his deeds came to an end at the Battle of Stainmore (although sources conflict about this event) and he was killed and buried. The worn stump of Rey Cross by the A66 is thought to be his grave marker (although it was moved from the South side of the road to the North in 1990) but his body has never been found.

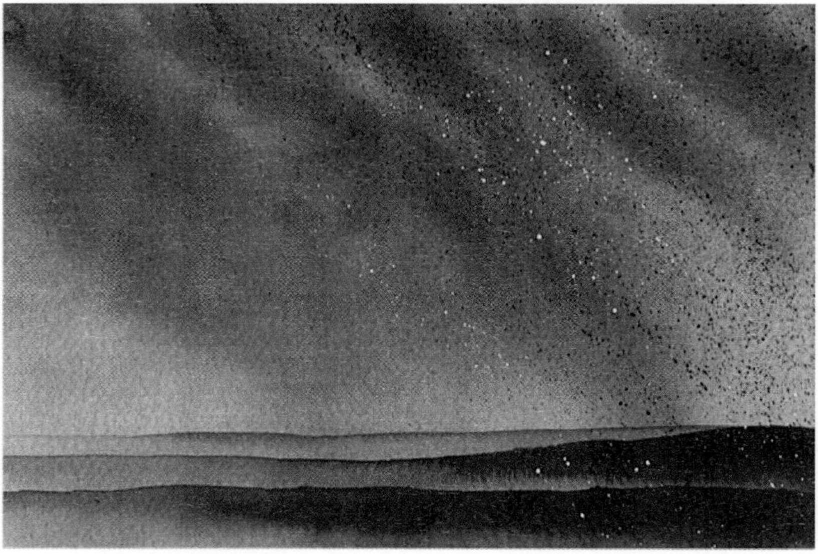

Rain on the Moor

The Roman Gold of Bowes Castle

The road running through Bowes village is now a quiet street but this used to be the A66 – a major trans-Pennine artery. This road is very old. A host of tracks, lanes and hollow ways converge on Stainmore Pass and the most important of them lies under this village street. This is the road the Romans made to stretch from Scotch Corner, leaving the eastern road for Scotland, to Penrith, where the western road for Scotland heads north.

The massive Norman keep which still guards the road is a later addition but it sits on a Roman fort.

This story is of a summer night, when two men, who had waited for many nights, were to have their patience rewarded. They were joiners – old friends who shared a workshop – and had grown up with this story:

> *Once upon a time some Roman soldiers were garrisoned where the castle stands, in the days when Bowes was called Lavatrae. The time came for the Roman soldiers to return to Rome. But they were wicked men and decided to plunder every village in the area before they left, so they stole all the jewellery and gold they could find and put it into a chest. They intended to take the chest home to Rome and retire as wealthy men. Then word came that the villagers had banded together and were coming to Lavatrae to seize their possessions. So the Roman soldiers buried the treasure.*
>
> *The following night the castle was attacked and the Romans were slaughtered but, of course, the treasure was nowhere to be found. However every year, on the anniversary of the event, the soldiers, in ghostly form, reappear and bury the chest again.*

The two men sat and watched late into the night. The first hint of morning was gilding the horizon when a group of ghostly men walked silently through the solid wall of the Norman keep with a heavy chest. They quickly and efficiently interred their luggage and their insubstantial bodies dissolved in shreds of mist.

The joiners moved forward stealthily with their spades, and dug until a pleasant hollow thud was heard. Quickly they disinterred the chest and carried it to their workshop.

It took a very short time for the more criminally minded of the pair to realise that sharing means halving. A well-placed chisel, slipped firmly into a ribcage, did its work very effectively and soon the treasure had only one owner. He decided to wait through the long summer day before making his departure at nightfall.

Time passed and, as it did, the surprised eyes of the dead man seemed to follow the living with an accusing stare. Flies gathered to visit the departed joiner. A lot of flies. The wall clock ticked, louder and louder, as the hours tiptoed by. At last, his heart beating double time, the sweat pouring over his face, the murderer knew what he must do.

When night fell he buried the chest – still unopened – and went down the hill to the deepest pool of the river. He filled his pockets with stones and walked into the water. After a while the bubbles ceased to disturb the surface.

The gold is still there for the taking, visited annually by the ghosts of thieves

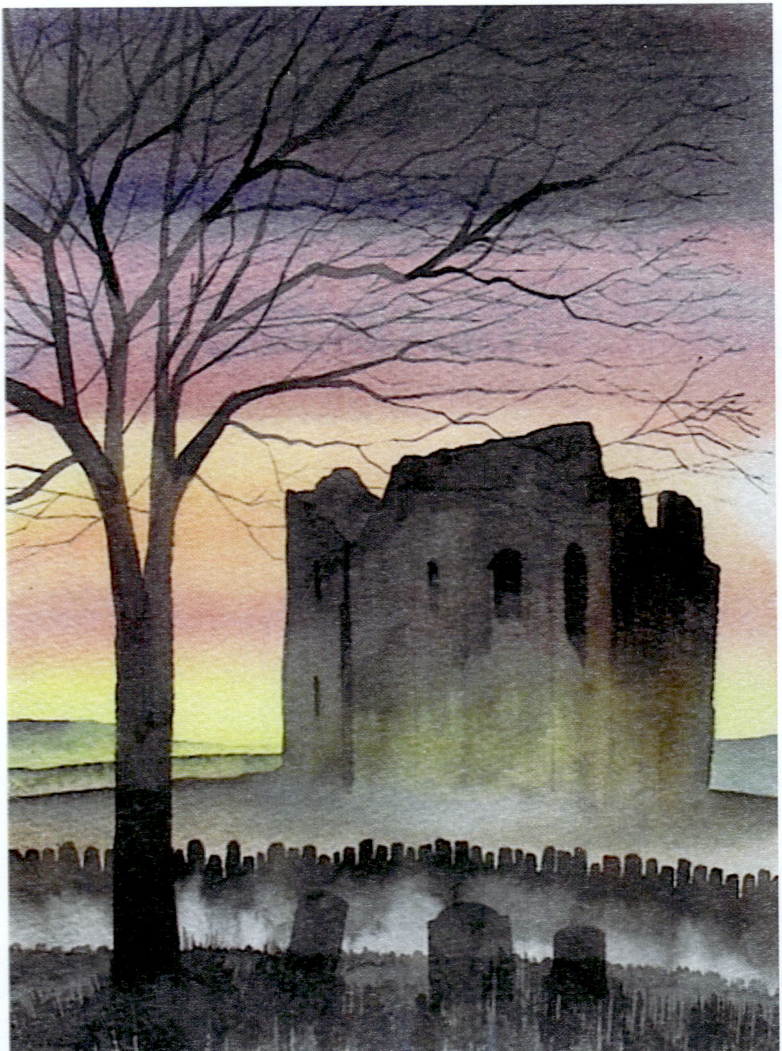

Bowes Castle, from the Churchyard

The Bowes Lovers

An Abstract From The Parish Register of Bowes:

" Roger Wrightson, Junr. and Martha Railton, both of Bowes, buried in one Grave. He died of a fever, and upon tolling his passing-bell she cried out ' My heart is broken,' and in a few hours expired through Love. March 15, 1714. Aged both 20 years."

In Bowes, on March 12th, 1714 , Pancake Day - Shrove Tuesday – tragedy struck on the doorstep of Spring.

In The King's Head, Roger Railton, the son of the landlord and landlady, was wracked with a fever. He was no fool, and could see his end fast approaching. He asked, he begged, he pleaded to see the woman he loved, of whom his parents strongly disapproved. Thankfully compassion won the day and his beloved – Martha Wrightson, whose parents kept The George Inn – was allowed to see him.

For months they had been meeting in secret against their parents' wishes, falling deeper into love, and forging a bond that would extract a mortal price.

Wednesday and Thursday passed and Roger sank deeper into the fever until Friday dawned and he died. Word was passed to the sexton of St. Giles church who sadly trudged to the church door. Once inside he unhitched the bell rope, grasped the sally and began the toll: one ring of the bell for each of the twenty years of Roger's short life. As the last note of the tolling bell rang out over Bowes Martha cried "My heart is broken" and in a few hours she too lay dead. Laid forever in a single grave they passed into death as they wished to have lived – together.

There is a beautiful plaque at their grave made by Bowes artist, John Degnan, which tells this story.

The Unicorn at Bowes has a reputation for being haunted by the two lovers, a twelve year-old boy who appears in the cellars and a bearded man in a bowler hat.

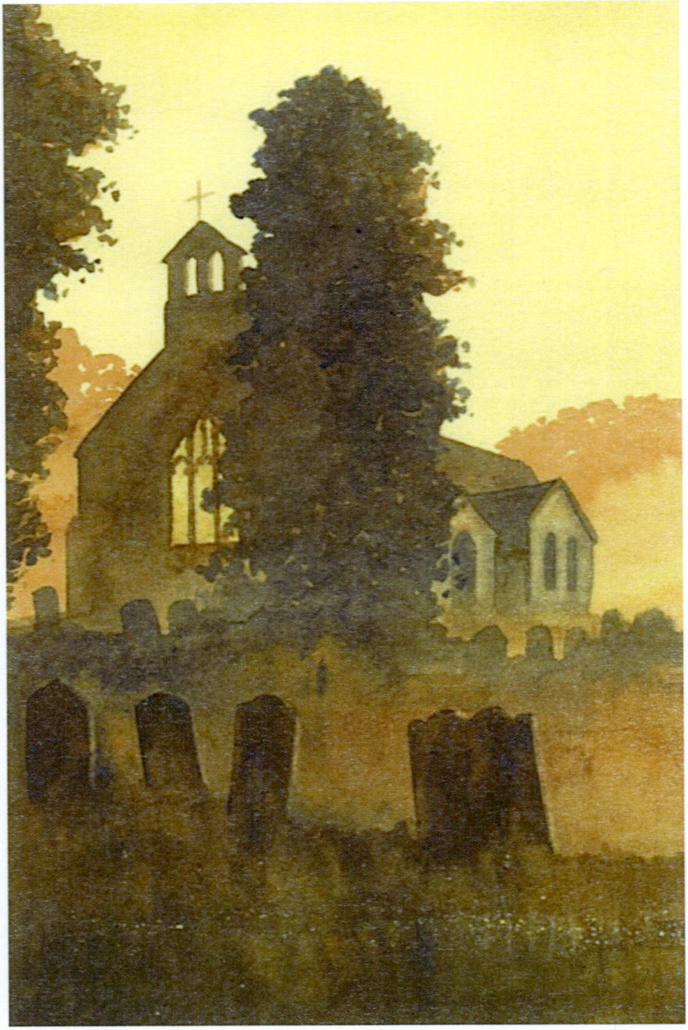

Bowes Church

The Road to Tan Hill

The road to Tan Hill is a great trip. After leaving Reeth you pass the turning for Langthwaite. This little village found fame after the bridge here was featured in the opening credits of the TV series *All Creatures Great and Small*. A little further along the road is a large church – huge, it seems, for the tiny village. The explanation is that Swaledale's population crashed as the twin effects of increasingly mechanised farming and the death of lead mining saw hundreds of people leave the Dale. Gunnerside's enormous chapel also bears witness to this phenomenon.

The next stop on the road gives a glimpse into lead mining history. The CB pub takes its initials from Charles Bathurst – Oliver Cromwell's doctor and the purchaser of Arkengarthdale in 1656. The Bathursts exploited the lead found here until 1911 when the falling price for the commodity put the final nail in the lead coffin. Part of their legacy is the Powder House of 1725 that stands in a field beside the road. Because of its structural integrity (lots of angled cornerstones), the octagon was better suited to contain an explosion than a square building.

As you gaze around you at this point the scenery is marked with a wealth of scar tissue. High up on the fell are quarries which produced chert and Yorkshire slates – the most common roofing material in these parts. You can see the ruins of lead mining storehouses and smelt mills and, here and there, evidence of hushing. This technique involved damming a stream, letting the water build up, and then releasing the flood. This would wash away the topsoil and reveal exposed lead veins. A shockingly destructive process which disfigures the Dales to this day.

And yet this still looks like paradise. The atmosphere of this lovely valley completely overrides the surface blemishes. It is stunningly beautiful.

As the road winds up towards Tan Hill the views to the North lengthen. Cross Fell and the ridges of Teesdale and Weardale become clearer until you can see all the way to Scotland.

Arriving at Tan Hill is the climax. The moor here is studded with shafts and drifts where the anthracite, or crow coal as they called it here, was dug for generations. It was still producing when the General Strike of 1926 shut the nation's pits. However the "blackleg" miners of Tan Hill toiled on.

These days Tan Hill is a stop on the Pennine Way and a gathering point for weekend tourists. The views are fabulous and the Tan Hill Inn, England's highest pub, is always busy. Since 1995, it has also had a licence for couples that wish to marry at high altitude.

Built in the 17th Century as a hostelry for coal miners, the Inn has accumulated at least three spirits. There is a silent little boy who appears, a secret smoker in the cellar who leaves behind the aroma of his (or her) last cigarette and Mrs. Peacock. This last one was landlady here for forty years and is seen whenever alterations are being made - presumably to see that they are being made according to her tastes.

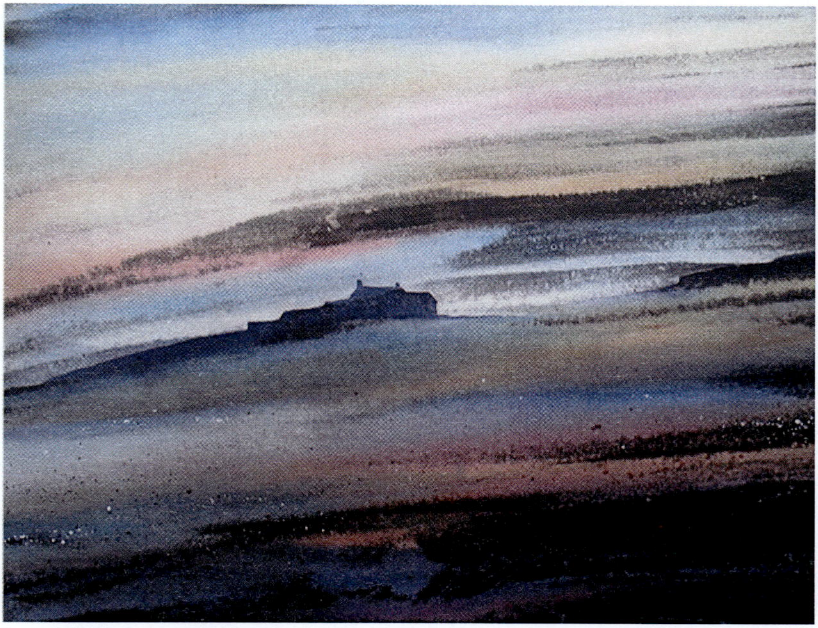

Tan Hill Inn

Pendragon Castle

Pendragon Castle is a place of many legends. It stands on a man made mound – the hill (Pen in Celtic) – in which a dragon is supposed to live. The first castle was built by Uther Pendragon, the father of King Arthur, and was held by him until a Saxon enemy managed to gain access to the well and poison the water, resulting in the death of Pendragon and one hundred of his men.

One of the castle's many owners was Sir Hugh de Morville. Sir Hugh was at Henry II's side when, exasperated by his one-time friend Thomas a Becket, the Archbishop of Canterbury, the king uttered the fatal words: "Who will rid me of this turbulent priest?"

With three other knights Sir Hugh travelled to Canterbury and confronted Becket. The Archbishop, who was about to join his fellow monks for vespers, refused to accompany the knights to Winchester to account for his actions to the King. He was then brutally slain.

As the aftermath of Becket's death sent shockwaves through England and beyond, Sir Hugh took his fellow knights to his castle of Knaresborough. He and the other assassins were not arrested, nor were their lands confiscated, but all four were excommunicated and required by the Pope to do penance. Sir Hugh could find no peace at Pendragon Castle. The silhouette of the neighboring Wild Boar Fell resembles the outline of a recumbent man and in that form he believed he saw the accusing profile of the dead Becket.

He finally did penance by travelling to Jerusalem to confess his sins at the cradle of Christianity. His ghost, along with that of Uther, continues to haunt the castle.

Pendragon Castle has another interesting legend attached to it. It is believed that a hoard of treasure lies buried in the ruins. Any attempt to uncover it, however, is hampered by the spectre of a black hen. As fast as any soil is removed the black hen replaces it.

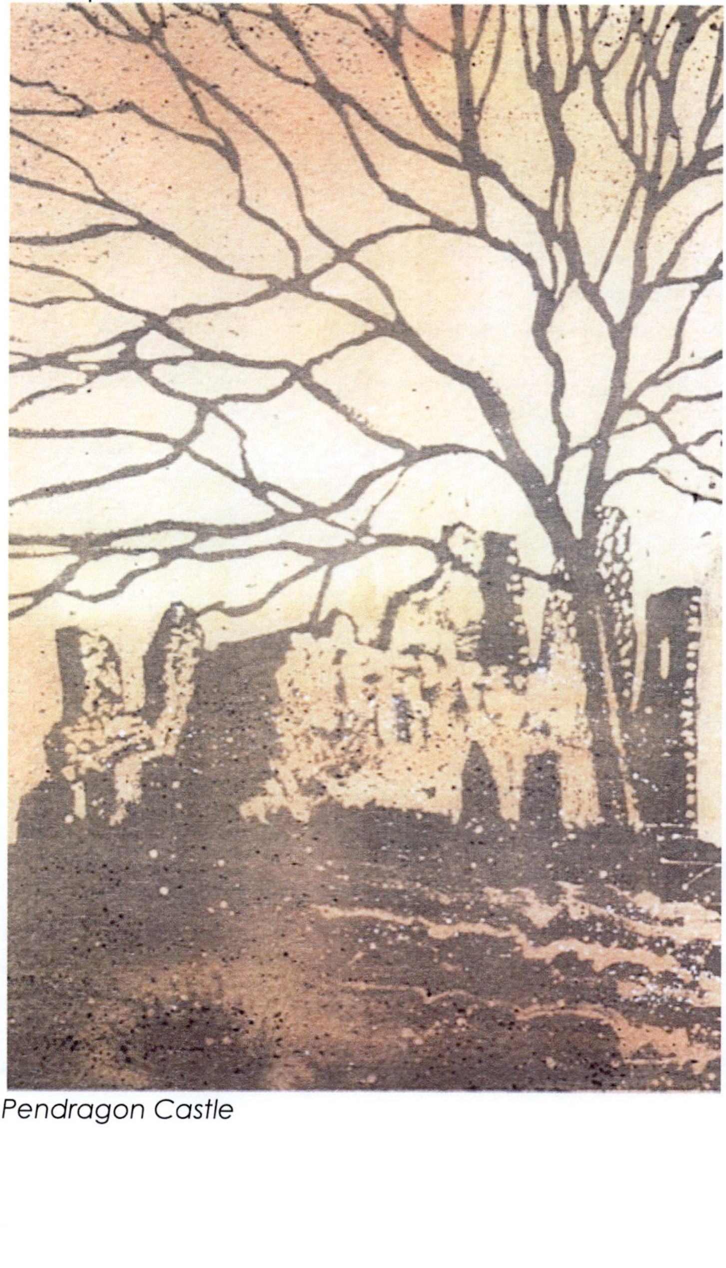

Pendragon Castle

Wild Boar Fell

In Kirkby Stephen church – which is just off the map as far as this book is concerned – is a tusk from the last wild boar killed in England. It supposedly died on Wild Boar Fell, one of the most dramatic hills in the Pennine chain. The fell has steep, stepped crags, sweeping, curved ridges, an outcrop quarried for millstones and a profile like no other hill in the chain.

On the Nab of the hill is a cluster of cairns. There are the Stone Men of Wild Boar Fell. Like the complex cairns on nearby Nine Standards Rigg, no-one knows why they were built. Theories include a guide to navigation or a stone army to deter invaders from Scotland. But nobody knows.

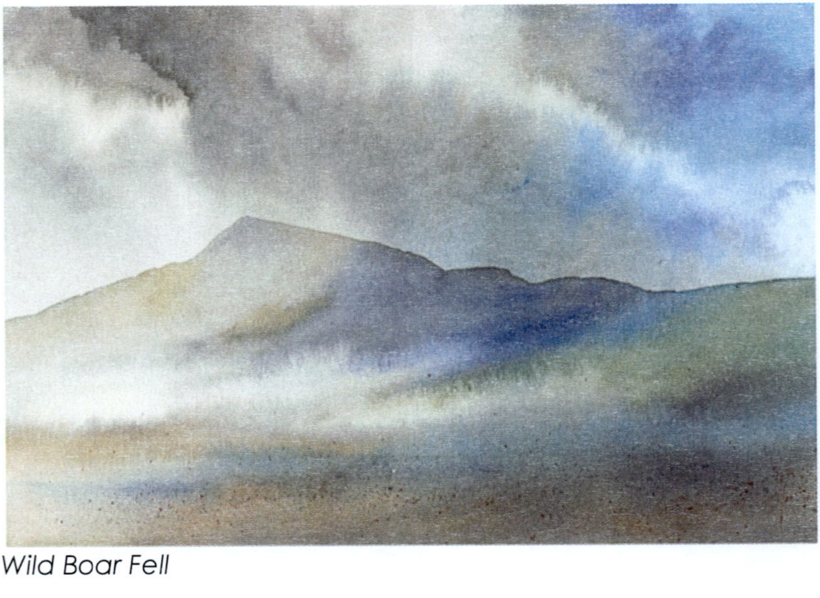

Wild Boar Fell

Hawes Junction Railway Accident

Industrial disasters have largely passed the Dales by. A lack of substantial coal mines, enormous factories and major roads have helped keep the body count pretty low. A notable exception to this was the Hawes Junction accident that was the result of a simple case of human error. One man forgot the time and two others didn't follow the rulebook. The results were tragic, especially since this took place on a Christmas Eve.

Incidentally, Hawes Junction was renamed Garsdale station after the line to Hawes and Northallerton from the Settle & Carilse Railway was discontinued. The signal box – the scene of the crime, so to speak – is still there on Garsdale station platform and continues to function.

On 24th December, 1910, in the small signal box at Hawes Junction station, Mr. Sutton, the signalman, was looking into the darkness beyond the row of brass levers. The rain was lashing at the glass and the sounds of engine whistles were lost in the noise of the storm. A little while earlier he had changed a signal so that two light engines could make their way northwards towards Carlisle but he forgot to change it back to warn any traffic that that section of line was in use. To make matters worse the engine drivers themselves, out there in the storm, didn't follow regulations in reminding him, preferring to stay out of the rain.

Eventually there was a distant rumble from South. The wet shining rails quivered, the ballast beneath the track began to vibrate and distant lights showed through the falling veil of water. In no time at all, with a burst of crimson, steam and brass, the Scotch Express thundered through the station.

A few moments later the driver of a southbound train for Leeds pulled up at the platform and ran to the signal box, the words tumbling out: that he has passed two slow moving engines a little way up the line. And he has seen the express heading, at high speed, onto the same rails.

The signalman couldn't believe the unfolding events. Before taking any action he scanned the pages of his train register, the awful truth dawning on him

When he finally lifted the telephone to call the signal box at Ais Gill this was the exchange:
Have two light engines passed north?
No.
Has the express passed?
No.

Mr. Sutton turned to the engine driver and said: *Go to the stationmaster and tell him that I am afraid I have wrecked the Scotch Express.*

Beyond Moorcock Tunnel the express ran into the two engines and was completely derailed. In addition to injuries caused by the collision, the timber-bodied coaches over-shot the ruined engines and the pipes for the carriage gas lights fractured. This resulted in a dreadful blaze as the coals of locomotive fireboxes ignited the gas. In addition to the large number of serious injuries twelve people died.

The area where this happened is one of the most remote sections of railway in England. Ais Gill is the highest point of the Settle & Carlisle Railway at 1,169 feet above sea level. You can see a panoramic view of the scene from the Garsdale to Hawes road, looking north towards Wild Boar Fell. It is hard to believe that something so terrible happened in a place of such beauty.

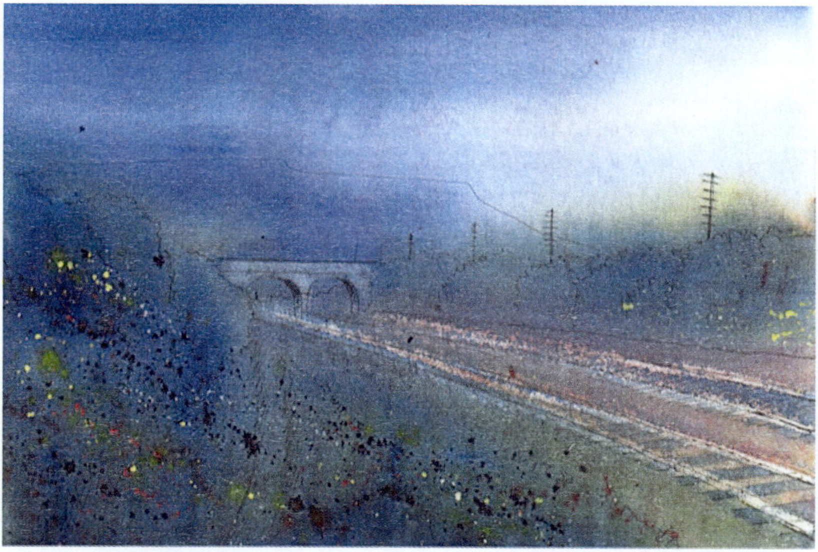

Ais Gill Summit

T'Auld Man

Miners comprise a superstitious workforce. In an occupation carried out entirely in an alien environment it pays to be as careful as possible. A miner either meeting a woman or a pig on the way to work should return home immediately. A crow perched on the mine entrance requires a similar action.

Once underground there is something that can keep luck on the miner's side. Many Dales house (including ours) have a hag stone hanging at an entrance. This is a stone with a hole in the middle, hung from a piece of rope. In the tunnels of Dales' leadmines small hag stones known as luck stones hang from the roofs of tunnels to keep the miner safe.

But the miner is never alone in the darkness. Wherever he goes T'Auld Man has been there first. Tapping away in the dark he commands respect and, almost, veneration. Lead seams do not run flat and predictable as do coal seams. The molten metal has settled in the cracks and crannies of the limestone and may follow all kinds of crazy routes, but the tapping of T'Auld Man has been known to lead to new, workable seams. Alas sometimes he leads to worked out seams, but this only adds to his acknowledged wisdom.

His closest known relatives are the Knockers – the miners heard tapping in the darkness by Cornish tin miners as they leave the pit at the end of a shift.

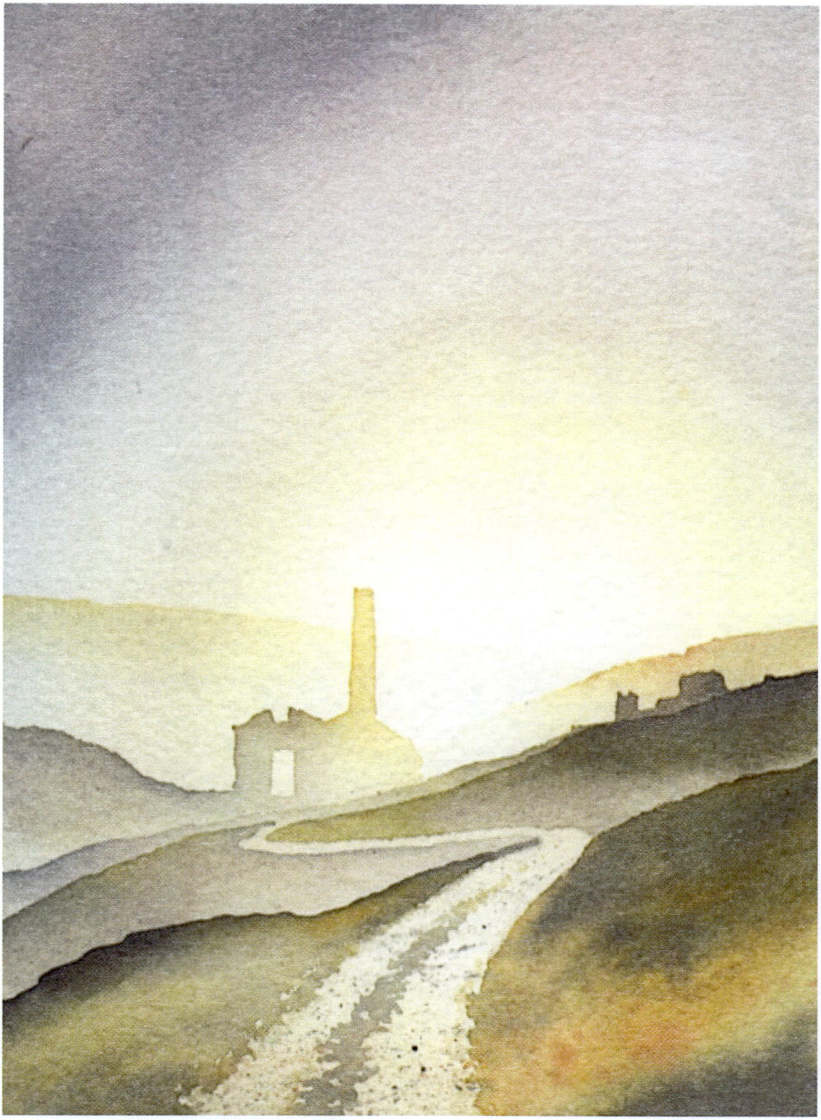

Old Gang Mines, Swaledale

The Swaledale Corpse Way

A Corpse Way in a path or road which was used when the time came to carry a body to consecrated ground. There are at least three of these in the Dales, and the best known is the one in Swaledale. The Corpse Way runs from Keld – the highest village in the Dale – to Grinton, which, for a long time, was the closest consecrated ground where a Christian burial could take place. To bury a body anywhere else would have condemned the soul to Hell and Damnation.

In 1580 a burial ground was consecrated at Muker, where a chapel-of-ease was built, and the Corpse Way was less used.

The Way begins at the tiny village of Keld. Keld takes its name from *kelda* – a Viking word for a spring - and water is everywhere around here. The Coast to Coast route passes through and follows the Swale through Kisdon Gorge with its lovely waterfalls, particularly Ease Gill Force.

In 1789 a travelling preacher turned up called Edward Stillman whose sermons were so popular that the villagers asked him to stay. There was a drawback: they had no church. He therefore decided on a plan to raise the cash – a sponsored walk. He set off and walked to London and back, raised £700 and the Keld Chapel was built. He stayed for forty-eight years and, when the church needed extending, put his boots on and did it again.

Keld was also the home of Neddy Dick, a nineteenth century musician who created a *lithophone* . This was a sort of marimba made of stones (mostly limestone from the River Swale) which were arranged on a frame and played with a pair of hammers. He got the idea one day when walking down near Kisdon Foss. His foot dislodged at stone which clonked musically against another as it rolled down the slope. He then spent hours collecting and refining his stones, chipping away to improve the tuning, until he had the perfect set.

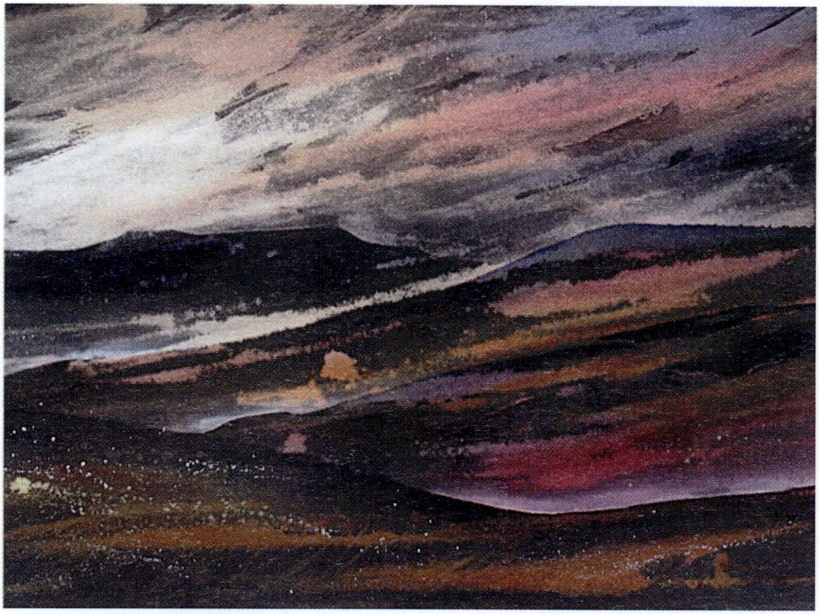
Looking from Kisdon Hill

The Corpse Way takes a route to the right of the green bulk of Kisdon Hill and swings toward Thwaite. This side of the hill is where the Swale once flowed until it broke through a new channel of the other side.

Before Thwaite comes into view the Corpse Way drops down the hillside. After all the effort the traditional group of four bearers must have made in getting up the hill with the dead weight in its wicker basket, it must have been galling to lose height, since they would have to get over the hill before the next village.

Thwaite was home to two pioneers of wildlife photography – Richard and Cherry Kearton. Born in the 1870s, Cherry and Richard were educated at Muker School, just down the Dale. They were fascinated by the possibilites of capturing wildlife on camera and, by 1896, had travelled to St Kilda and the the Outer Hebrides to photograph birds.

Cherry went into wildlife movies making *Roosevelt in Africa* and *A Primitive Man's Career to Civilisation* in 1910 and 11.

They pioneered the use of a disguised camera in a novel way. Made of an ox's hide, canvas and wood the Kearton Ox was a strange beast – a fake cow from which the brothers could photograph wildlife.

Whether this is the origin of the term "hide" as a photographic term I've no idea.

From Thwaite the Corpse Way climbs back onto Kisdon Hill and, passing some old mine workings on the summit, drops down to Muker. The views are amazing – Wild Boar Fell, Buttertubs Pass and the whole of Swaledale.

In Muker The Queens Head was a traditional resting place for the corpse and the bearers would be refreshed with beer from a special set of funeral mugs.

At Ivelet, a little further down the Dale, there is a flat stone by the river. The Corpse Road forded the Swale here before the bridge was built, and the stone was a resting place for the coffin. It is thought there were several of these on the route but I suspect the rest are now doing service as lintels, gateposts or fulfilling some other recycled role.

Ivelet also has a ghost – a headless dog. The creature runs up the slope onto the bridge, leaps the parapet and dives into the river. It is an ill omen, foretelling death. This must have been less than comforting to the pall bearers.

The sixteen-mile Corpse Way was a two day affair. The four bearers were paid a fee which covered an overnight stop at the Punch Bowl Inn in Low Row and, hopefully, for a few pints of beer. Meanwhile the corpse rested in the Dead House, a small, square building by the Corpse Way on the hill above the pub.

The route to Grinton crossed the river near Reeth and passed near a substantial earthwork. This is Maiden Castle. This was a Brigantian stronghold of Queen Cartimandua. In AD 69 she, and her consort Venutius, were allied with the Roman legions but, shortly after, the two divorced. Venutius led a campaign against the Romans which failed, but not before he had created the enormous series of ramparts at Stanwick.

Maiden Castle also has a buried treasure. Many people have tried and, apparently, one group dug a shaft and actually found the chest. Unfortunately a black hen then appeared, flapping her wings and putting out the light. The treasure hunters returned the next day to find heavy rain had caused the shaft to collapse and they were unable to relocate the goods. So it's still there...

The Corpse Way finally ends at St. Andrew's Church, Grinton, known affectionately as "the Cathedral of the Dale". It's a real beauty inside and out – a twelfth century gem with a Jacobean pulpit and a "squint" so that lepers could watch the mass from outside the walls. Here the corpse would end its journey and the bearers would return up the dale until the next time.

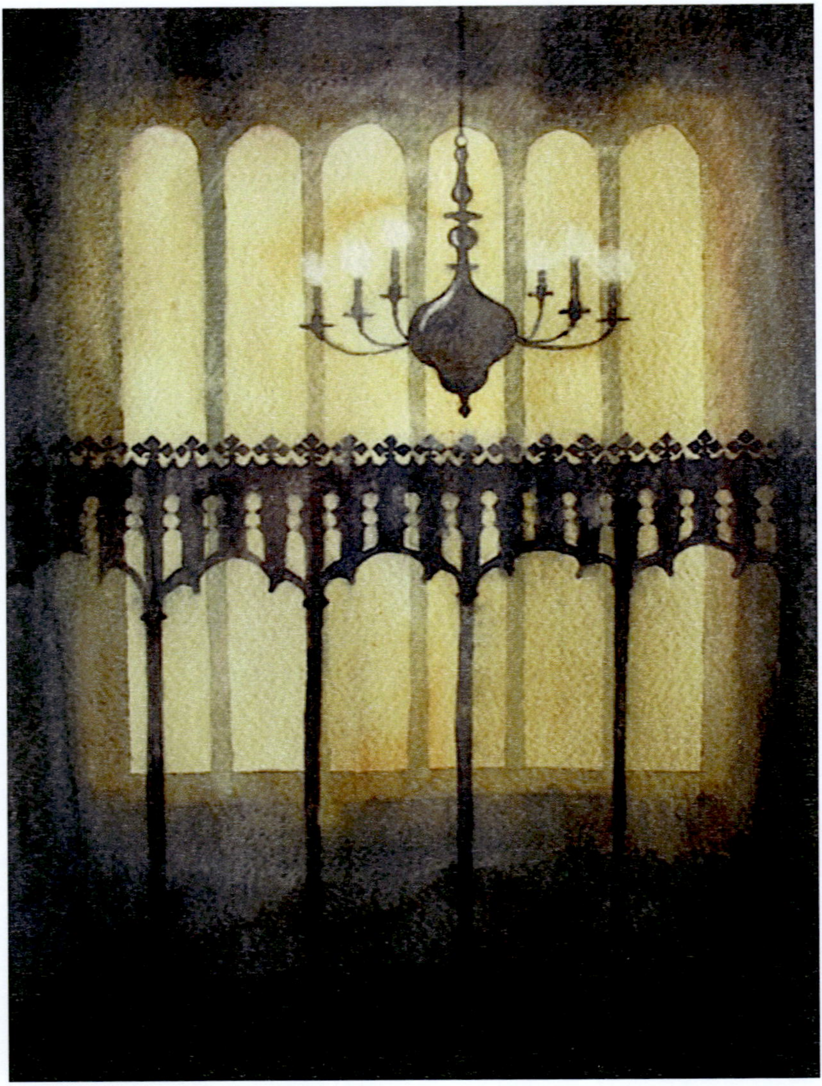

Grinton Church

James Herriot's Conversion on the Road To Reeth

Like a lot of people who love the place, my appreciation of the Dales was greatly enhanced by the writing of a Sunderland-born vet. Although he worked from a practice in Thirsk, Alf Wight, who the world got to know better as James Herriot (he took his pen name from the Scottish goalkeeper Jim Herriot), spent a lot of time here. He sometimes worked with a practice partner based in Leyburn and, when he married, chose Coverdale for his honeymoon.

The films and television episodes that followed the success of his books featured many Dales locations and today, over forty years after the publication of his first book, countless people come to the Dales from around the world to find what he found.

Everyone who has read these charming stories has probably placed them in particular favourite Dales locations but, for me, it was in his autobiographical Dales journey *James Herriot's Yorkshire* that he made me look at a place that sums up the Dales.

He tells of how he suddenly saw a sight that stopped him in his tracks, and made him realise that the Dales had everything he could ever wish for in a landscape. And in that moment he knew he would never live anywhere else.

If you take the road for Reeth out of Leyburn you pass, as you leave the town behind, a rather grotty quarry on your left and a boring pine plantation on your right. Then the landscape begins to open up but, instead of driving out onto open moorland, you find yourself passing firing range after firing range where the army has literally put the boot into Yorkshire.

Once you come to the end of this dispiriting area, however, something wonderful happens. The road crests the brow of the hill and there before you is the view which converted Herriot to the Dales.

To the right, far away, are the Cleveland hills and beyond them the chemistry sets of Teeside, looking like tiny toys in the sunshine. To the left are the heather heights of Grinton Moor, studded with the ruins of the lead mining trade, splashes of green grass marking the places where the rabbits have carved out their grazing rights.

Ahead is Swaledale: farmhouses dotting the valley floor, dry stone walls climbing the fell sides, and hills and ridges marking away the miles to the North and West. It is incomparable.

Thank you James.

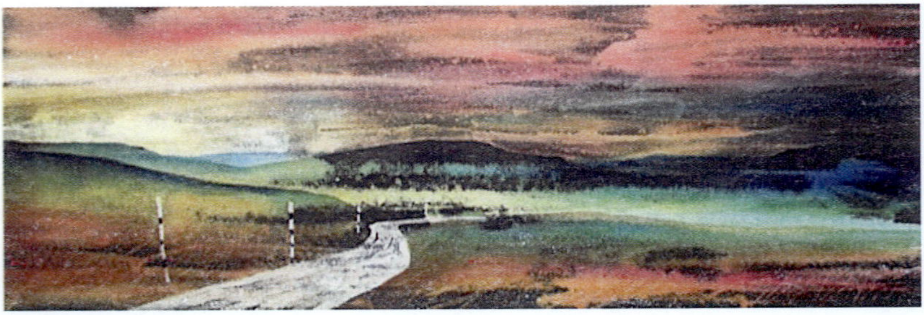

The Road to Reeth

Willance's Leap

In 1606 Robert Willance – a Richmond draper and lead mining entrepreneur – was riding home along the high ground on the North side of Swaledale. It was a very misty day and he was counting the ditches he had to jump his horse over and lost count, and lost his way. Coming to a break into the ground he assumed he was at the edge of one of the ditches, spurred his horse forward and jumped.

As he waited to land he probably realised he had jumped over the cliff edge. He fell two hundred and twelve feet and, miraculously, survived. The horse wasn't so fortunate.

He had badly broken his leg and, until help arrived, kept it warm by cutting open the horse's side and inserting his leg into the animal's stomach. The leg eventually had to be amputated. According to tradition his leg was buried in Richmond churchyard and, when he died, the rest of Robert went to join it.

A succession of stones and inscriptions have marked the point where he leapt.

It's a good story, and part of it is echoed in other tales. Rob Roy, the Scottish hell raiser, is supposed to have hidden from his pursuers by cutting a hole in a dead cow and, in the *Star Wars* spin-off, The *Empire Strilkes Back,* Han Solo cuts open an animal's body to keep Luke Skywalker out of the weather.

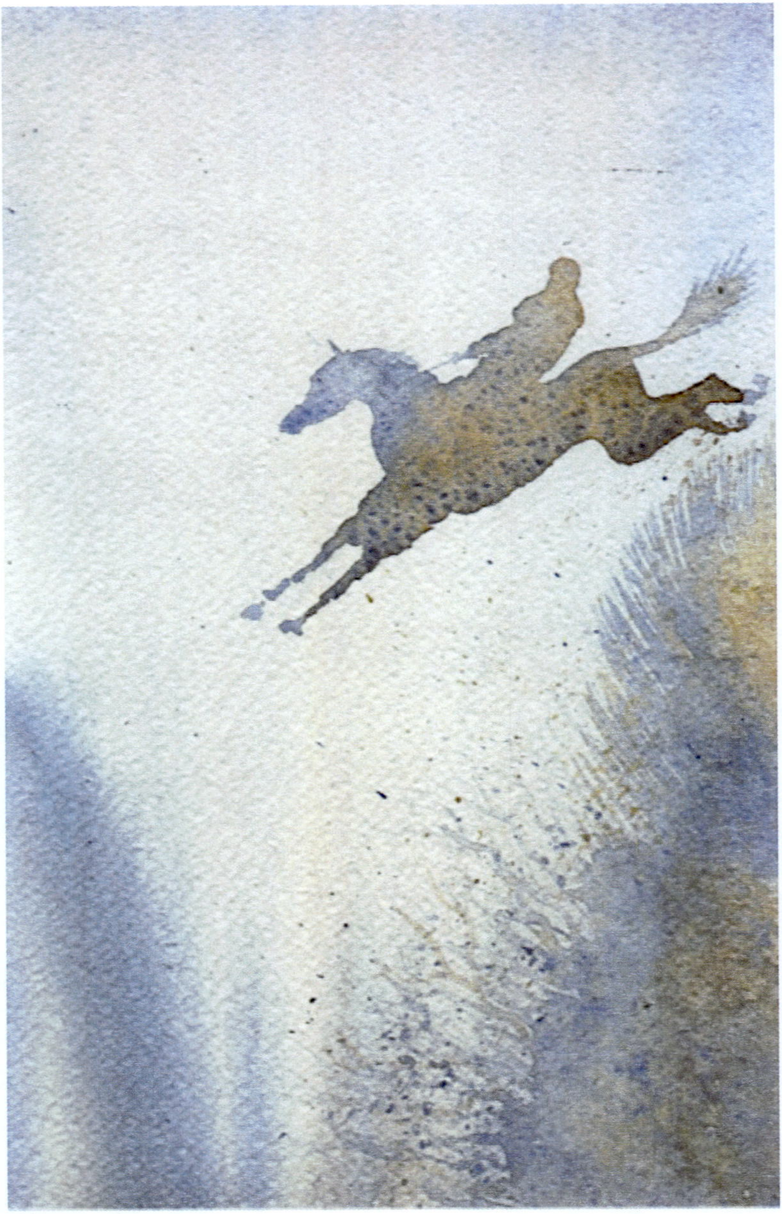

Willance's Leap

Potter Thompson

Richmond Castle, and indeed most of the town, stands on a great outcrop of rock on the doorstep or Swaledale. The peaty brown waters of the river curve around the rock and pour over the falls and away to the Vale of York. A walk on the castle terrace or along the road at the foot of the rock emphatically impresses on you the massive weight of limestone above your head. And somewhere in this wall of rock there is an opening.

At some point in the eighteenth century a potter by the name of Peter Thompson went for a walk. It is said – as it is so often, probably unfairly, said in tales – that he had left home to avoid the nagging of his wife. The fact is that if your job involves handling mud all day which, when dry, covers you, your home, your larder and your loved ones in a layer of terracotta dust then you are unlikely to win a popularity contest. Whatever the circumstances of Thompson's domestic arrangements, he went for a walk he would never forget.

In a cleft in the rock he saw a cavern opening before him and, in the far distance, a pale light. He stepped into the darkness. The long passage broadened out into a huge chamber and, dimly, Thompson could see the dust shrouded forms of armoured knights reclining on plinths of stone. In the centre of the chamber was King Arthur, asleep like his companions of the Round Table, with a horn and the sword Excalibur by his side.

Drawn irresistibly to the famous weapon, the trembling man reached out his hand and touched the gilded hilt. With a gentle, insistent pull, the sword began to slide free of its scabbard, the untarnished blade gleaming in the shadows.

But with a distant rumbling, which became a squeaking of old iron and rose to a rusty clatter, the sleeping knights began to stir. Thompson froze, his hand holding Excalibur, with the sword halfway in darkness and halfway in light.

There was a mechanical creak, terrifying loud in the echoing cavern, as every armoured helm among the company of knights turned his way. As a cold chill raised the hairs of the back of his head, Thompson's courage deserted him and his hand left the sword. Raising clouds of dust from the chamber floor he ran for the distant entrance and heard, ringing from the cavern walls, these words:
"Potter Thompson, Potter Thompson,
If Thou hadst drawn the sword or blown the horn
Thou hadst been the luckiest man e're born."

Of course, once the terrified man stood blinking in the daylight turned to look back at the rock wall, the cleft had closed.

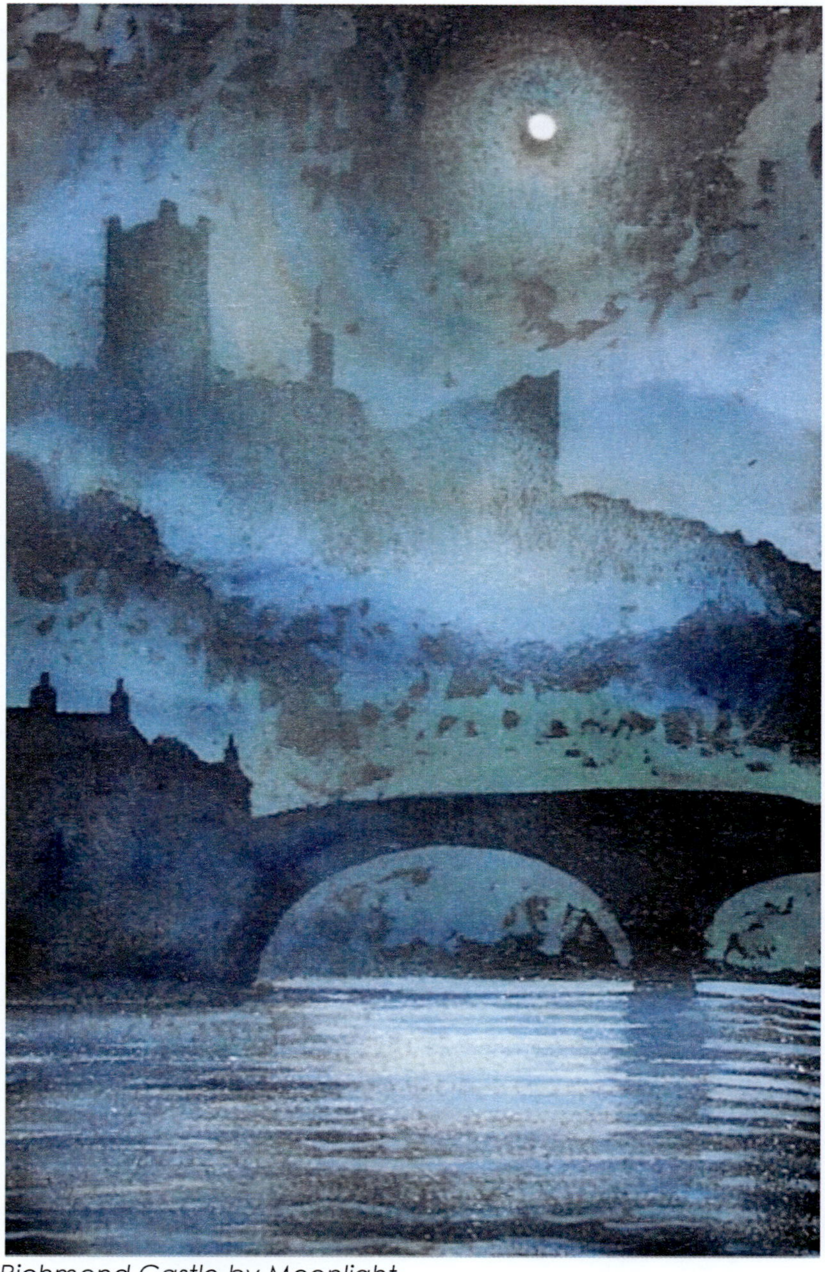

Richmond Castle by Moonlight

The Drummer Boy

It is a Sunday in the barracks and the soldiers are bored. A few are playing cards, some smoking and some are talking about the town where they are garrisoned. Richmond has been an army town for a long time and the stories are handed from one company to another, growing and changing as different tongues shape the stories in their own way. A man is telling a story, a legend about the cavern beneath the castle where kind Arthur is sleeping. His companions, for want of something to do suggest a search of the cellars and so, with lanterns in their hands, they explore the deepest chambers underneath the Norman keep.

A small doorway is found, a doorway which none of them has noticed before. The passage beyond is so small that no soldier can fit into the space. They pause, light their pipes and discuss the next move in their campaign. When they have drawn up their plans the drummer boy is called for. He is given a lantern, a promise of wonderful rewards and a gentle shove to start him on his way. Under orders, he beats his side drum, the percussive waves of sound pouring into the darkness.

Above the ground the soldiers, stepping quietly to catch the sound, follow his regular beat. Through the town he leads them and turns to the South East, keeping to the left bank of the river. The ruins of St, Agatha's Abbey at Easby come into view and the rattling snares on the drum continue to mark their steps and then....

And then nothing. The sound abruptly stops. They look at each other and at the ground, as if it might speak and offer some explanation, but there is none to be had. They return to the castle and call into the darkness but no reply comes. For a day or two the tiny door is left ajar, but the boy is gone and will never be seen again. And so the door is closed, locked, and never reopened. And over the spot where the last drumbeat sounded the drummer boy has a small memorial of grey stone.

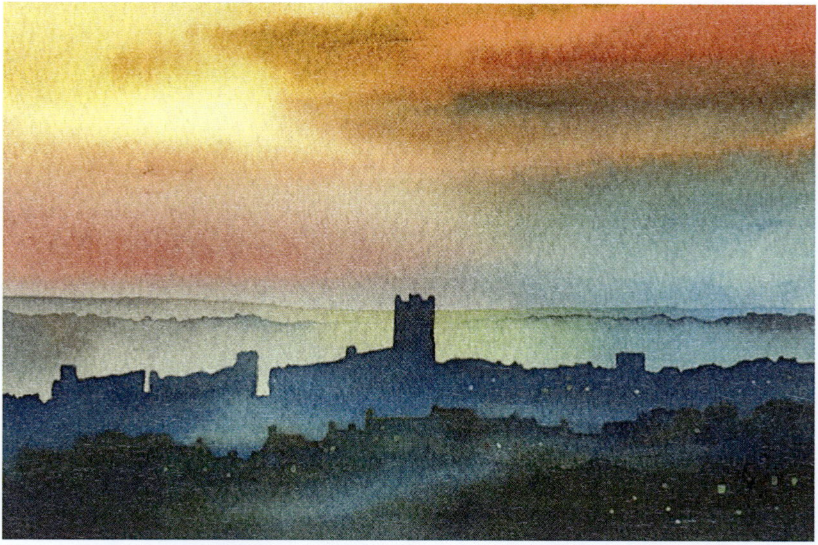

Richmond from Maison Dieu

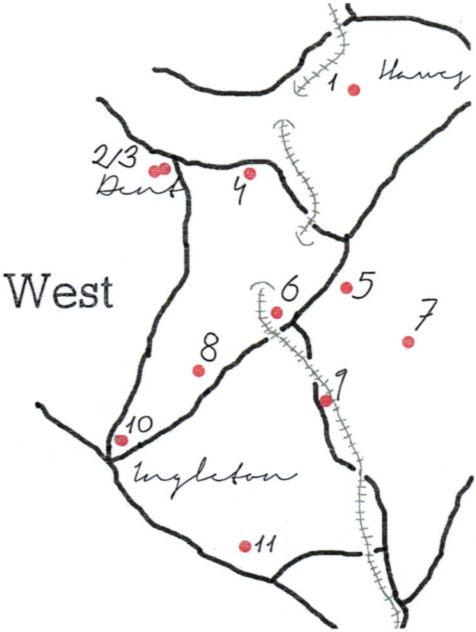

1 Galloway Gate
2 The Fall & Rise of George Hodgson
3 Adam Sedgwick
4 The Witch of Ibbeth Peril
5 The Gearstones Fairies
6 Railway Stories
7 The Barguest of Cam Houses
8 St Leonard's, Chapel le DaleThe
9 Empty Tins, Selside
10 The Ingleton Money Tree
11 Witch of Clapham That Never Was

Galloway Gate

Galloway Gate (from "gaten": a Viking word for a road) is an old drovers way, one of many in the Dales, crossing the hills at the end of Dent Dale and Garsdale. Its mostly a ridgeway, as such ways are known, following the high ground and keeping the cattle away from lowland bogs, village streets and other obstacles.

The name comes from a type of packhorse – the Galloway pony (often called a Gallower by Durham miners, who used them as pit ponies). Much of Galloway Gate is now a tarmac road but there are still parts which are just a broad track, settled slightly into the ground by constant use. This allows you to step out of time and just walk under the broad sky as people have done on this road for two or four or more thousand years.

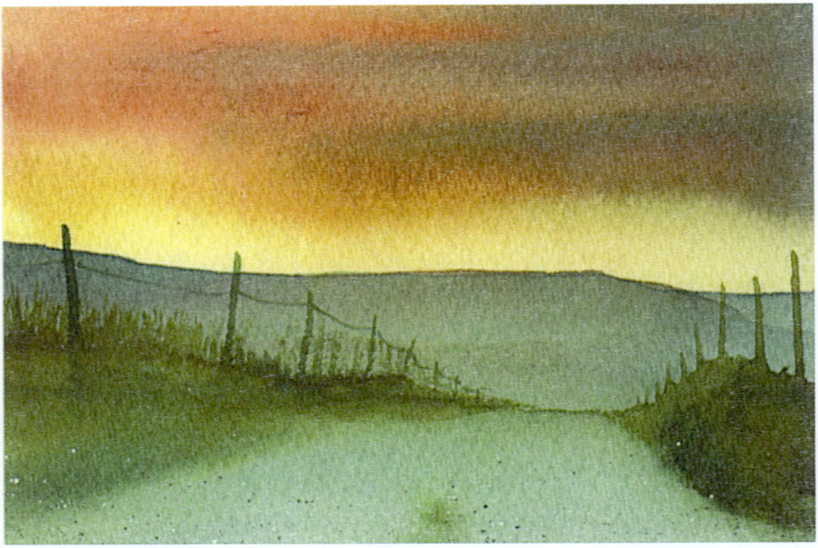

Galloway Gate

The Fall & Rise of George Hodgson

In 1621 Galileo invented the telescope, the Mayflower sailed from Plymouth and George Hodgson was born in Dentdale. In 1715 James Stuart set in motion the Jacobite rebellion, Handel watched the premiere of his *Water Music* and George was buried in a corner of Dent churchyard.

That should have been the end of the story but, surprisingly, George began making regular appearances in and around Dent. The Dales are full of eccentric characters but this was undoubtedly more eccentric than usual.

Stories began to circulate about George's previously blameless life. A "friend" recalled that George enjoyed a daily glass of sheep's blood as a tonic. A neighbouring farmer put about the story, shamelessly lifted from an old witch legend, that he had seen a black hare one day. Raising his gun he had shot and wounded the creature, followed its bloody trail to George's door where, surprise, surprise, he had looked through the window to see George tending a shotgun wound.

There was a lengthy town meeting and a decision was taken: to exhume George and then take whatever action was deemed appropriate. Accordingly the sexton and his spade were summoned to the churchyard and, after some effort, George's coffin was brought to the surface.

The interiors of used coffins are rarely attractive and George's was no exception. His skin was pink and healthy, his hair and nails had grown somewhat but he was undoubtedly dead – though not sufficiently dead for the citizens of Dent.

A new grave was dug at the church door, a stone laid and a brass stake driven through the corpse. The top of the stake is clearly visible. As a result of this treatment George has ceased to reappear - so far.

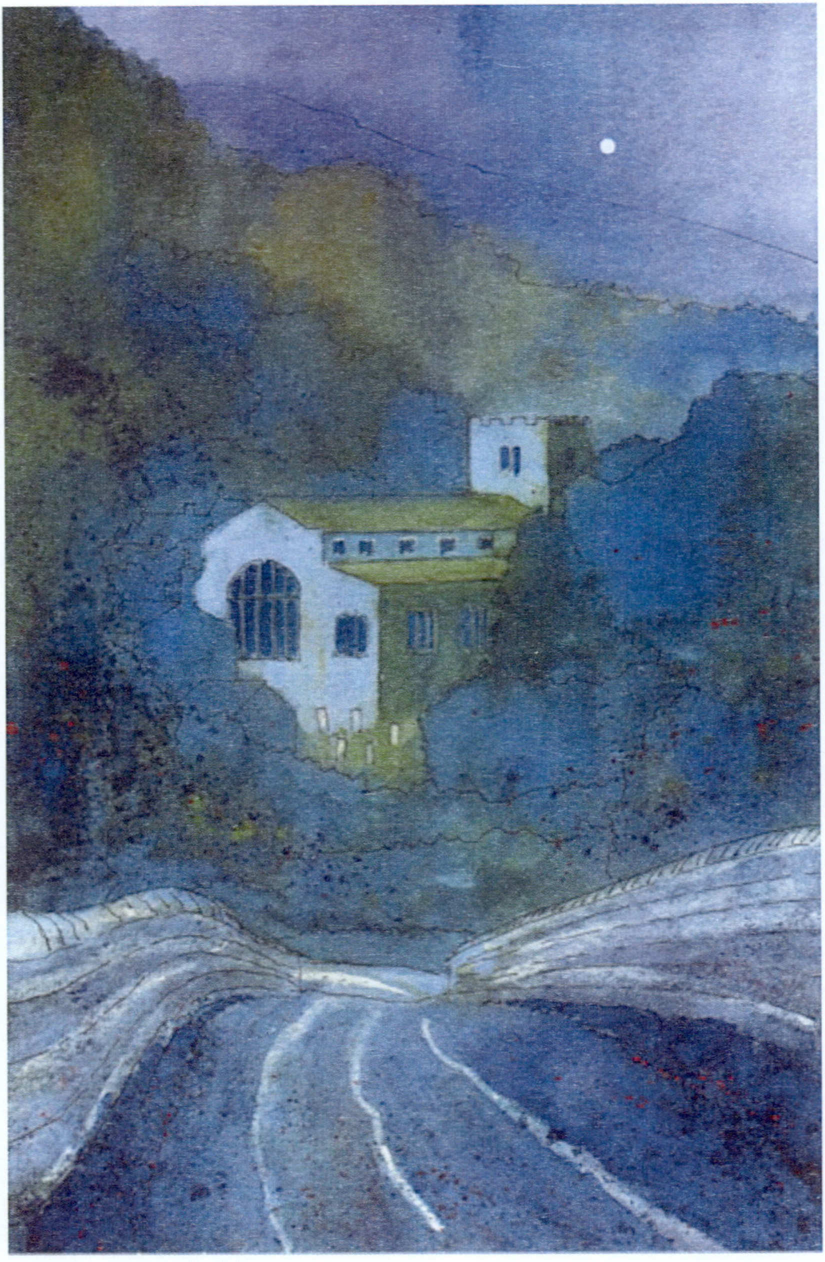

Dent by Moonlight

Adam Sedgwick

In the centre of Dent is a large rough stone which stands near the entrance to the churchyard. It carries the inscription "Adam Sedgwick 1785-1873".

Sedgwick was the son of an Anglican priest. He was a geologist and was born in this small Dales village. He had a distinguished career in which his greatest achievement was the beginnings of the modern classification of rocks. He proposed the Cambrian geological timescale after studying beds of Welsh slate. He probably had developed some ideas about this after looking around the Dales where, particularly at waterfalls, the layers of strata are clear to see.

Among his pupils at Cambridge, where he was a fellow of Trinity College, was Charles Darwin with whom, despite their differences, he maintained a close friendship all his life.

Sedgwick was a man with a dilemma. Religiously conservative, he had to marry in his own mind the discoveries he was making with his firm belief that all things were the creation of God. His belief in geological timescales was at odds with a church which had stated that the world and everything in it were no more than 6,000 years old. He became a national celebrity in the liberal press when, defending his beliefs against attack from the Dean of York in the Minster's chapter house, the entire chapter refused to sit down with him.

However his own Anglican beliefs led him to oppose Darwin's theories of evolution and natural selection and he wrote, in one case, that these were "utterly false". Unfortunately he is often remembered better for this than for giving the world an instantly-understandable interpretation of geology.

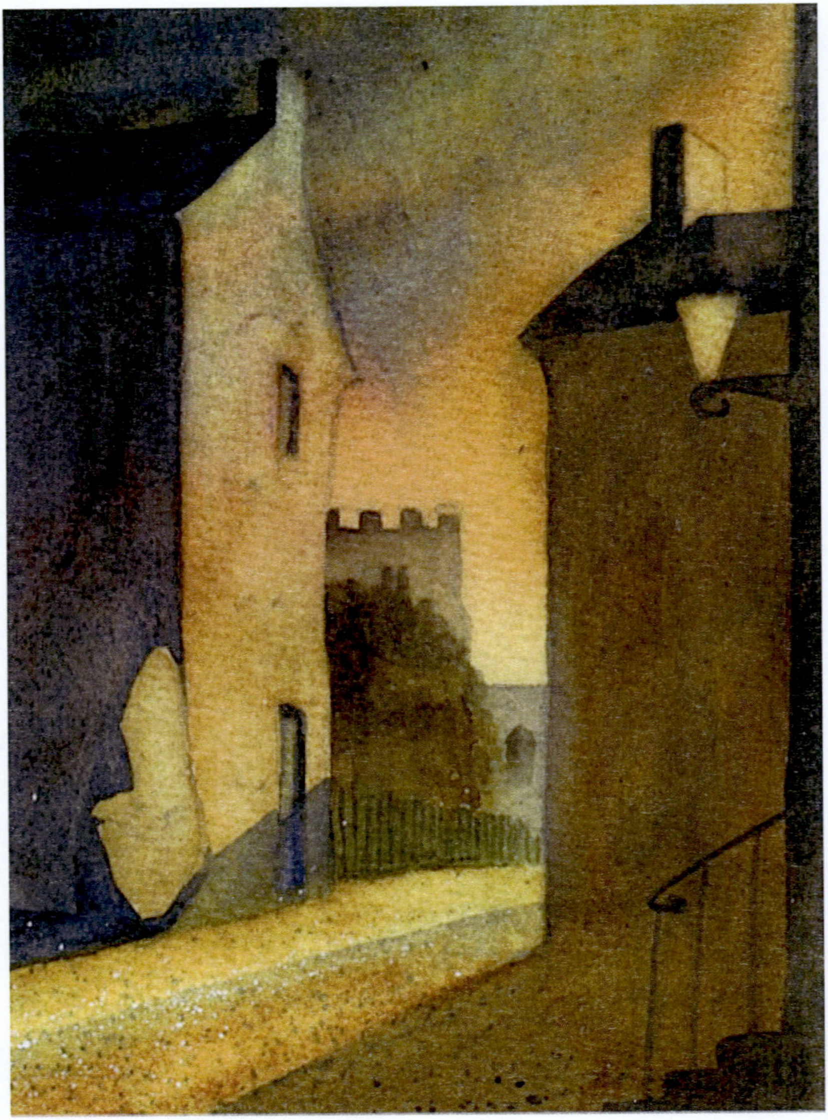

The Sedgwick Memorial, Dent

The Witch of Ibbeth Peril

In 1869 the Midland Railway started building the Settle to Carlisle line as a way of getting its passengers to Scotland. For years it had been frustrated by the London and North Western Railway who owned the West coast main line. The final ding-dong with the LNWR came when they wouldn't allow the Midland to use its station at Ingleton, resulting in two stations in one tiny town. The Midland had had enough and set out to build the line that most people said couldn't be built.

Now although the Settle Carlisle line is a spectacular and astonishing engineering achievement it lacks something in terms of customer satisfaction. This is because, like an early version of a budget airline, the stations are nowhere near the towns they are named after. So if you get off at Dent Station you'll have to walk four and a half miles to get to Dent.

(Fortunately they renamed Hawes Junction as Garsdale – it was twelve miles from Hawes!)

One benefit of the walk from Dent Station to Dent, however, is that it takes you through the beautiful valley of the River Dee. The river is pretty much invisible a lot of the time – heavily wooded and deep down in a gorge.

When I went to find the cave of Ibbeth Peril it was a damp autumn day. The leaves were thick on the trees, the brambles prickly and non-compliant and the rocks above the gorge were moss covered and slippery. I eventually found my way down to the riverbed by falling into it, after a brief, unplanned, but exciting journey, on my posterior.

I stood up, made sure that nothing vital had snapped, and found myself in a broad, deep, stone lined channel. There was no sky above – just a mass of trees - and there was only a slight trickle in the streambed. It seemed completely silent.

In the course of researching this book I've found myself in some extraordinary places but this took the biscuit. The whole pack of ginger nuts in fact! I walked until I found the cave. It wasn't hard. There is a lovely waterfall, a round pool of deep green water and, beside it, a big black hole in the rock.

The story goes like this: If you got drunk the witch that lived here would find you as you were walking home. While befuddled by drink she would lead you, with suitable seductive promises, to this gorge. If you were lucky she would lead you into a deep, deep cavern (which, by the way, is about half a mile in from the cave entrance), and leave you there to sleep it off. You would wake up, hungover and disoriented in the dark, with a mouth like the bottom of a witch's cave, and have to find your way out.

If you were unlucky she just drowned you in the pool.

The gorge is a very scary place. The atmosphere is cold and everything seems unnatural. It feels more like the surface of the moon that the Yorkshire Dales. You are acutely aware of being in a physically vulnerable position: in a water channel with plenty of evidence that sometimes the river here is a violent torrent. In fact a school party had to be rescued from Ibbeth Peril cave in 1990 when heavy rains made the river rise with frightening speed. The event led to a revision of safety procedures for parties going underground.

But who was the witch? There is very little known about her, but she seems to have been called Ibby, short for Elizabeth, and she's buried in Dent graveyard. Her fame only grew after her death, due to her cruel and unusual stand on binge drinking. Whether she exists or not, Ibbeth Peril is an amazing place, but next time I won't go there alone.

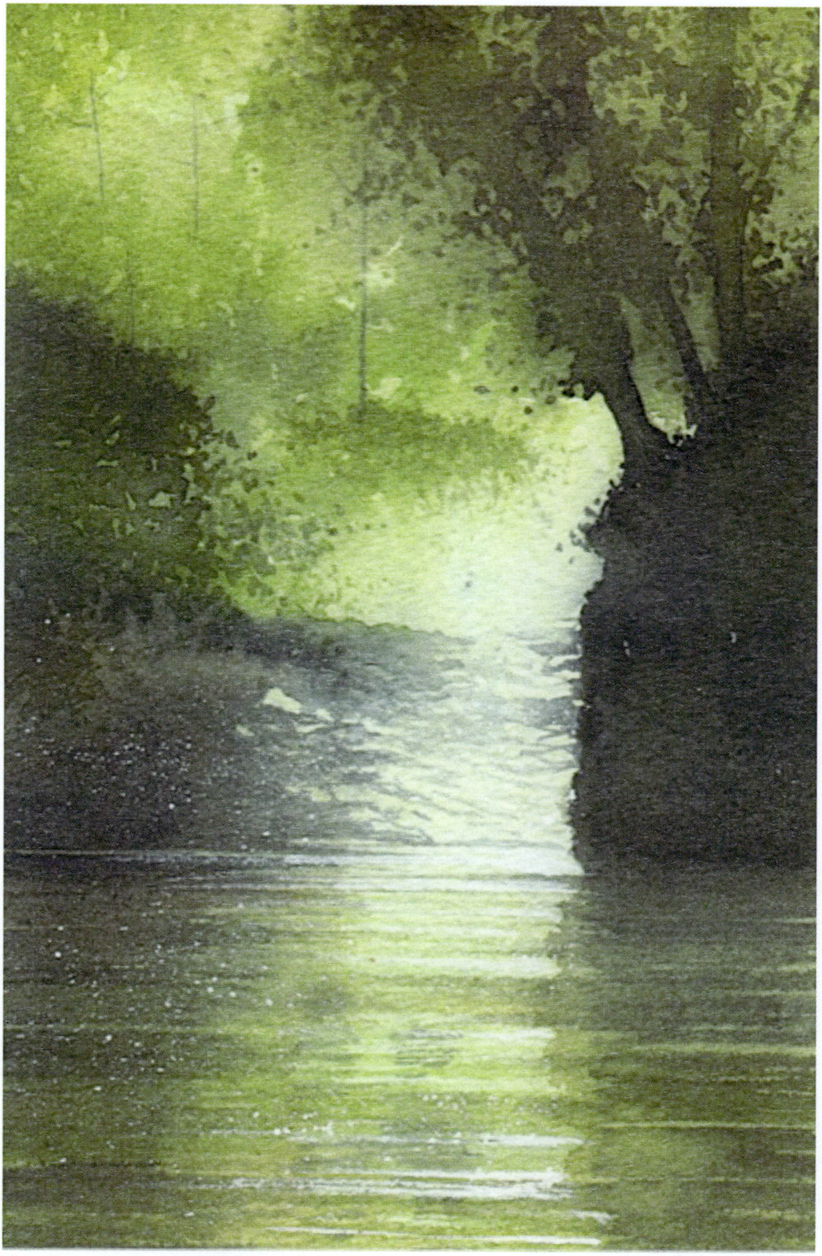

The Pool of Ibbeth Peril

The Gearstones Fairies

When I went down a pothole for the first time it was a brief trip of a few minutes. We walked into a cave called Calf Holes. I remember water flowing over my boots, the daylight disappearing and that once-sniffed-never-forgotton smell of carbide lamps. The stream rippled before us into the dark and I saw it fan out into the depths of the cave as it formed a waterfall.

Later the same day I made my first proper trip underground. I had a helmet but the rest of my gear consisted of a pair of borrowed wellies, a torch and a boiler suit. Despite the wet and the discomfort of crawling and contorting myself I was amazed by the other worldliness of the pothole. Over the next few years I went through some wonderful caves, learned the difference between stalagmites and stalactites (tites come down!) and saw things you couldn't see anywhere else.

Its not surprising that they are lots of stories to do with potholes, but this tale is very strange. The two men who told it to me promised to write down all the details and email them, but I never heard from them again.

Two cavers, with a passion of caving photography, went to a pothole at Geartsones, high on the plateau where Ribblehead Viaduct stands. They changed into their wetsuits, unpacked their gear and set off.
But once underground they found that, whatever they did, their floodlights and cameras stubbornly refused to work. Finally they gave up trying and just decided to go through the cave for fun, rather than waste the day, so they stashed their gear high above the water level and set off.

Now the cave was fairly full of water but it wasn't a fast flooder so they weren't worried about getting trapped. However there was a low duck in the cave where they would have to put their heads underwater briefly to enter the main chamber.

They were both experienced and negotiated the duck without a hitch.

When they got into the main cave, however, they immediately felt something strange happening. Around them they could hear, what they could only describe to me as "fairy music" – unearthly sounds ringing and echoing across the deep water in which were standing up to their necks. Simultaneously they felt a gentle, insistent force pushing them back the way they'd come. They were both convinced that someone or something was telling them that they weren't wanted. Without panic, but puzzled and slightly frightened, they retreated.

The next week one of them returned. After a few sleepless nights he'd convinced himself that he couldn't let this experience turn him against potholing and he had to face his fear. He went back to the main chamber and – nothing! Everything was calm. Mightily relieved he went home.

But a few weeks later he was back with a school party. The water levels were well down and the visit was exciting for the children but in safe conditions. In the cave he asked a little boy what he thought of the place. The lad paused and then said: "Its great, but I don't like the people in the rocks."

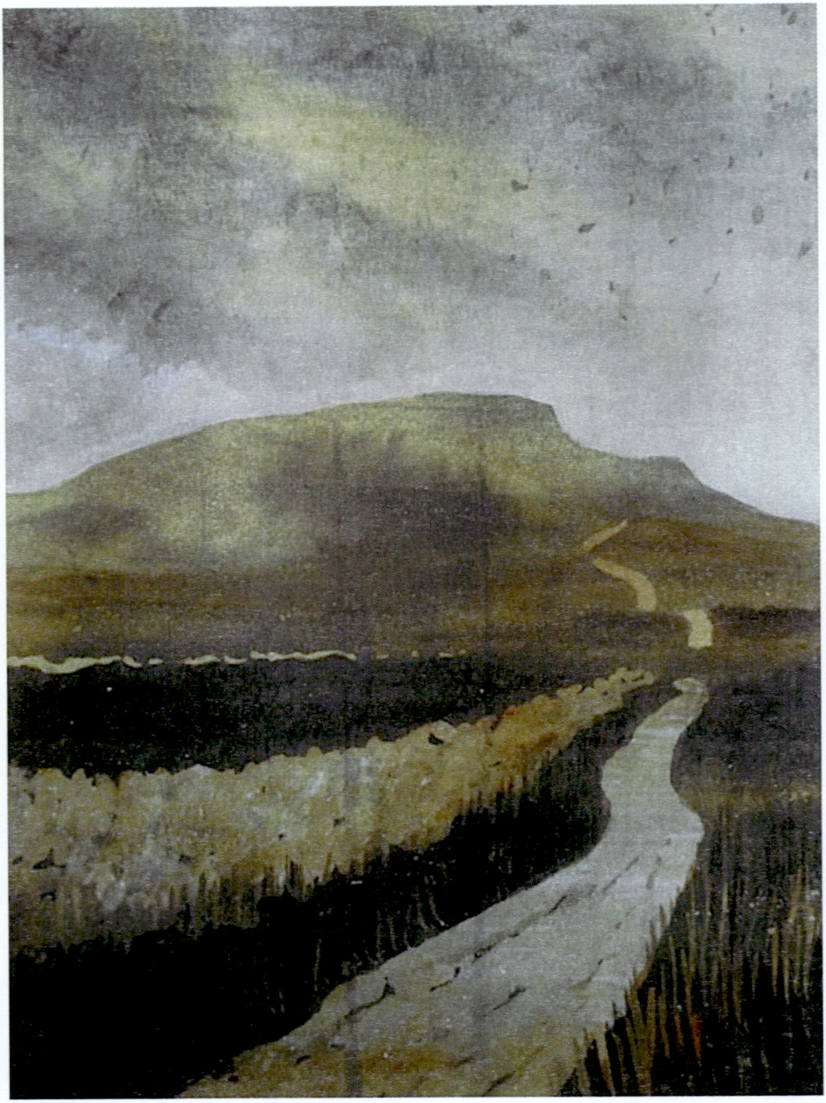

Penyghent

Railway Stories

Railways are a popular gathering place for stories and the Settle & Carlisle Railway has plenty. Here is a small selection.

I have known this first story since childhood. It was picked up by the Rev. W. Awdry and retold in the series of books that brought Thomas The Tank Engine to the public's attention.

At Garsdale station, which for a long time was known as Hawes Junction, there was a turntable. It was in a very exposed position – Garsdale is one of the highest points on the line – and the winds here can reach terrific speeds blowing a gale for days on end.

One day an engine was being turned to take some wagons down to Skipton. The wind was picking up nicely and was blowing against the flat-sided tender, pushing the engine round. The turntable began to pick up speed when, just as the tender came broadside to the wind, another terrific gust increased the pace. The watching railwaymen could do nothing but watch and wait until someone had the idea of throwing sandbags onto the turntable bearings. Eventually this did the trick and the engine was stopped. To prevent the same thing reoccurring a stockade of sleepers was built as a windshield that remained in place until the machinery was retired. It went on to have a second life (as well as a literary one) by being re-sited on the Keighley and Worth Valley Railway where it continues in use today.

The second story is one that crops up in a couple of other places where high bridges exist.

A driver and fireman were taking an engine across the Ribblehead Viaduct in a howling gale. Suddenly the driver felt his cap rise from his head and blow up high above the train. He watched it fall away and presumed that would be the last he saw of it when, from the other side of the bridge, his hat reappeared and plopped back down on his head. If this

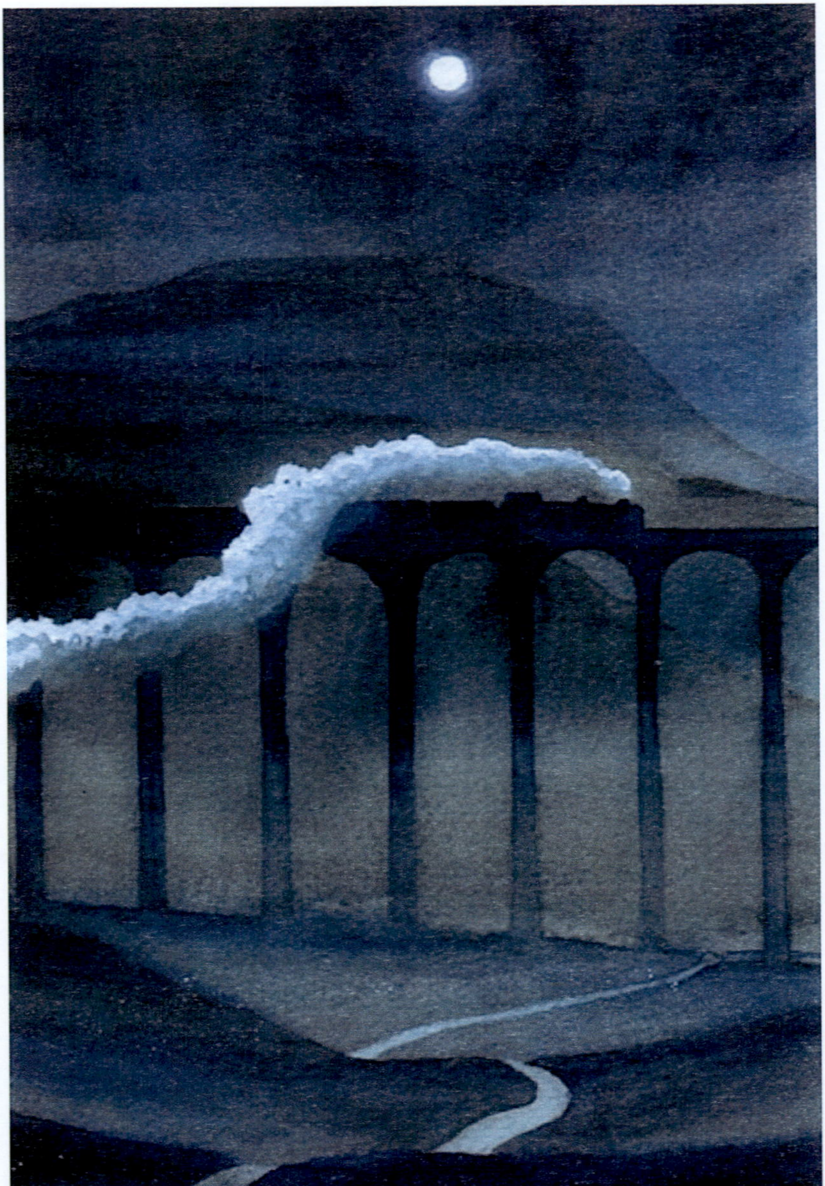

The Night Mail, Ribblehead

sounds too good to be true it is: the hat, on its reappearance, landed on his head the wrong way round.

The third story also cropped up in another place and time: Arten Gill viaduct is nowhere near as famous as Ribblehead but it's a cracker. With eleven arches, 117 feet high and 220 yards long it's a big building. Because of the terrain the pillars are of different thickness. It spans a deep-headed valley at the top of Dentdale. The viaduct, like many of the bridges on the Settle & Carlisle is made of a hard limestone known as Dent "marble" which was also used for decorative masonry because it's very pretty, being packed with fossils.

The quarries are very close to the viaduct and the track, Arten Gill Lane, which leads to them, under one of the arches, is a branch of the famous drove road Galloway Gate. The central arch carries a large stone dated 1875.

It is said that in this year that the daughter of a local farmer went missing. She had been sweet on one of the navvies who had been working on the railway and a love affair had blossomed. As time passed the viaduct foundations were nearly complete and it was about now that she told her lover of her pregnancy. He made all the right noises about asking her father for her hand, but forgot to mention that he already had a wife.

On the night that was to be their last meeting, they took a walk up Arten Gill Lane and he strangled her. He dragged her body to one of the foundation shafts of the viaduct and tipped her in, throwing some hard core down to cover her body. And so one of the pillars of Arten Gill viaduct is reputedly built on a sad story.

A strange echo of this tale occurred in the early 1960s. After the building of the M1, when the East London Kray brothers were carving out their criminal empire, it was said that one of their victims was encased in a concrete pillar holding up one of the new motorway bridges.

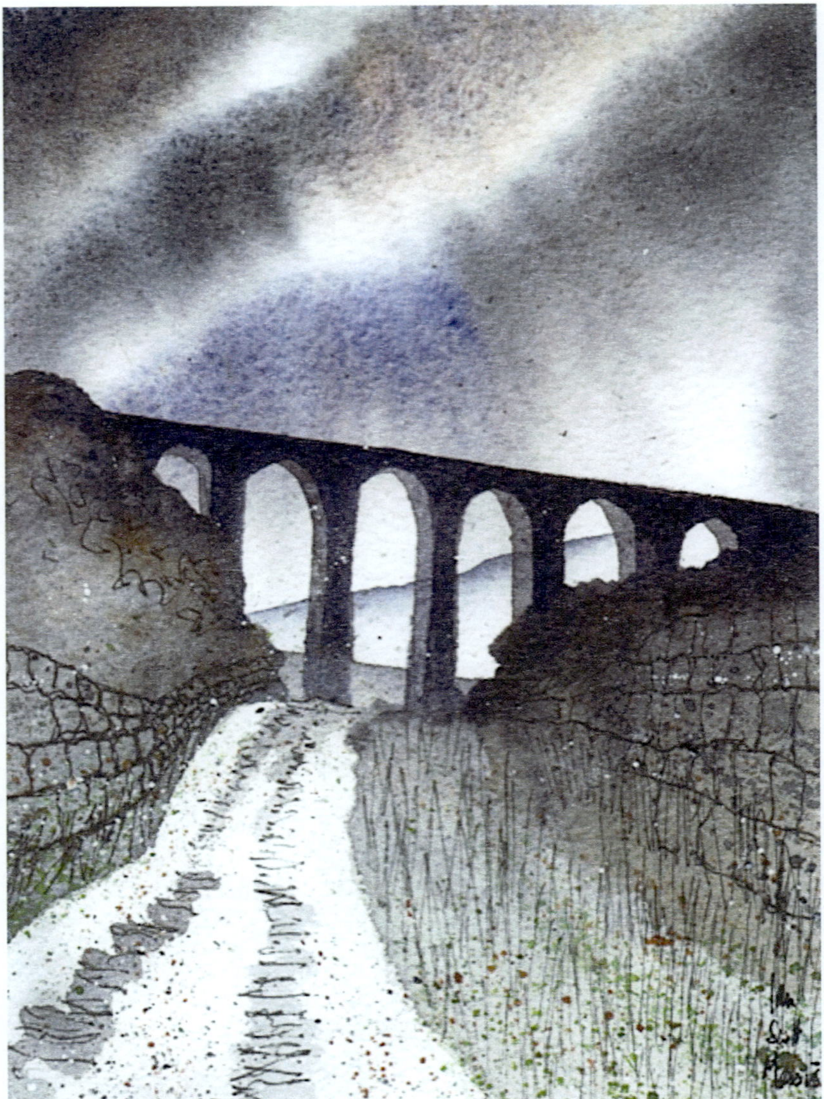

Arten Gill Viaduct

The Barguest of Cam Houses

The roads that run through the Dales have changed repeatedly over the centuries. The place where this story happens used to be a fairly busy route, but is now just a track for walkers.

There is a Roman road that cuts through the Dales from Ingleton to Bainbridge. As you leave Ingleton, heading up Chapel le Dale, you pass an area of open moor and then the road straightens up and runs like an arrow towards the Ribblehead Viaduct. Look over the dry stone wall to your right and you'll see what looks like a railway embankment climbing up the dale beside you. This section of Roman road is so well preserved it really looks like something from the nineteenth century.

When the Roman road reaches the Ribblehead plateau it leaves the modern road and becomes a track, and striking off toward Bainbridge's Roman fort, by way of the heights of Cam Fell. As it nears the highest point a smaller track branches off towards Upper Wharfedale. Both of these tracks were coaching routes two hundred years ago, and this gives you a pretty good idea of what the roads were like in the days before MacAdam.

This is the watershed. One stream running West from here, the Ribble, will meet the Irish Sea at Liverpool. A matter of yards away, another stream, the River Wharfe begins its long journey to the North Sea.

Just down the angle of the slope, as Wharfedale begins to open up, is Cam Houses. Its just a collection of farm buildings, stables and a derelict house now on the Dales Way, but for coach travellers this was a stopping point for changing horses, having a bite and spending a penny.

The old windowless house where travelers ate and drank is now a dark-windowed shell. This was home to the spirit known as Auld Joiner. Apparently benign, he would hammer and saw away happily, but always in the next room – heard but never seen. The other Cam Houses ghost also wasn't seen, but wasn't benign.Jenny or Jerry – different texts disagree – was a huge black, shaggy and invisible dog. Such a creature is known as a Barguest.[1]

People couldn't see him/her but horses could. Many a traveler approaching Cam Houses would find their mount trembling and refusing the stay on the road. The frightened horse would then flounder muddily in a wide circle to avoid the unseen hellhound before coming back to the track some way further on.

Whether the Barguest was responsible or not Cam Houses, was the scene of a sort of Yorkshire *Marie Celeste*. One day the coach came down the track to find Cam Houses deserted. Fires were burning in the grates, food was laid on the tables, but all was deathly quiet. The residents were never seen again.

I went to Cam Houses on a mizzly autumn day, approaching from the Roman road that runs along the ridge. Low cloud was all around me until, taking the turning to Cam Houses, I dropped out of the mist just before seeing the old inn. It was like something straight out of Hollywood and I could've believed in any number of ghosts, Auld Joiners and barguests at that moment. Definitely worth the visit, but the wait for a really grotty day before you go.

[1]See The Barguest of Troller's Gill.

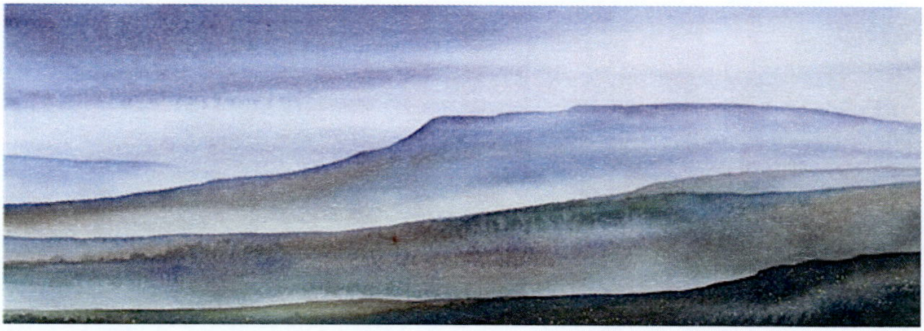
Cam Fell

St Leonard's, Chapel le Dale

The first mention of this little church is in the late 16th century. At some point it lost its name and was known as the Chapel for Ingleton Fells for a long time. Then, in 1940, a document from the 16th Century turned up establishing its original dedication and it's been St. Leonard's again since then.

There's a sad memorial here in memory of those who died in the building of the railway between Settle and Dent Head. Their fellow workers paid for the memorial. When smallpox ravaged the construction camps the churchyard had to extended to cope with the bodies.

Behind the church is Hurtle Pot, a slippery-sided hole in the ground that is best viewed from a distance. Nearly sixty feet down is deep pool in which black trout supposedly swim, and where a boggart likes to drown curious visitors.

Boggarts are most often found in stories about Dales houses. They can be very helpful if treated well (a bit of bread, cheese and beer now and then, basically) and will help out with light domestic duties: doing the dishes, bringing in the coal – that sort of thing. If they are crossed however you can look forward to sour milk, thrown pots and pulled hair.

There are stories of people moving house in the dead of night to evade a troublesome boggart only to find that the disruptive creature so and so has hitched a ride in the furniture.

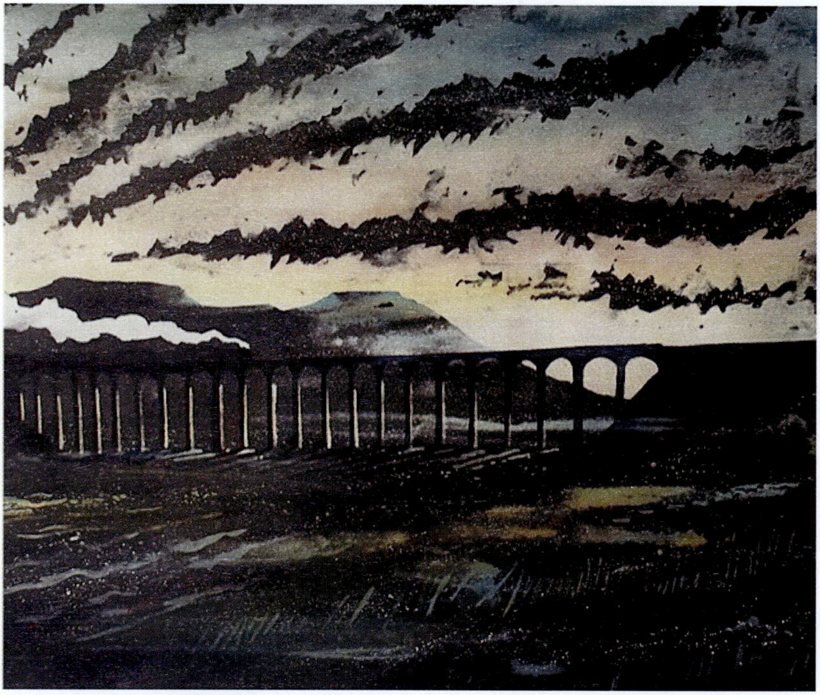

Ribblehead Viaduct

Empty Tins

There's a nice story about about Dales economics from Selside, It's a tiny village – blink and you've missed it. But if you're coming up from Horton in Ribblesdale towards the Ribblehead viaduct there's a little barn by the side of the road where someone, years ago, put up this lovely sign saying *Selside*. Its right in the middle of the Three Peaks and you get a gorgeous view of Penyghent all the way up that road.

Now there's a group of houses there that back onto the railway line and an old dear used to live in one of them, and she came up with a great way of keeping warm in winter.

Every time she had something out of a tin she would take the empty tin and put it on the back wall where the trains went by. Then, whenever one of the engines passed, the driver and fireman would chuck pieces of coal to try and knock off the tins. So then she would go out and, hey presto: free coal!

Of course the only downsides to this were that she had to remember not to put up the tins when she had her washing out, and she had to dash indoors whenever she heard a train coming to avoid get clobbered.

This is the Settle to Carlisle Railway by the way, where the very last British Rail steam train ran in August 1968, so this story has to come from before then. I don't know what she did for fuel when they changed over to diesels.

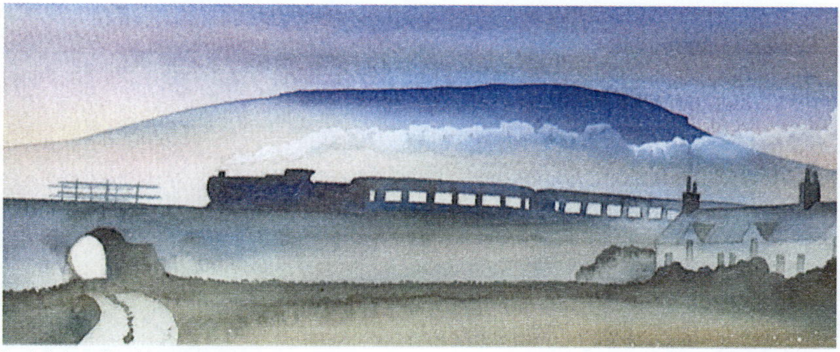
Selside Cottages

The Ingleton money tree

In 1885, with an eye to the blossoming tourist trade, Ingleton established a company to improve access to the remarkable series of waterfalls upstream from the Dales town. The result was a brilliant success and the walk, which takes in the falls is a perennial favourite.

Near the beginning of the trail is a tree that appears at first to be armoured. The Money Tree is studded with coins which have been hammered into the grain as a sort of local variation on flinging a coin into a fountain. No-one seems to have any idea when this originated but it seems to be a fairly recent development of an old idea. The evidence is that this tree, and the ones at Bolton Woods, Hardcastle Crags and Hebden Bridge appear to have no pre-decimal coins in them.

There has been a long tradition of tree decoration. It was quite normal at one time to tie gifts to trees for the spirits that dwelt within and there is a custom in Scotland of the Kissing Tree: if a man can drive a nail into a tree with a single blow he can claim a kiss from his sweetheart.

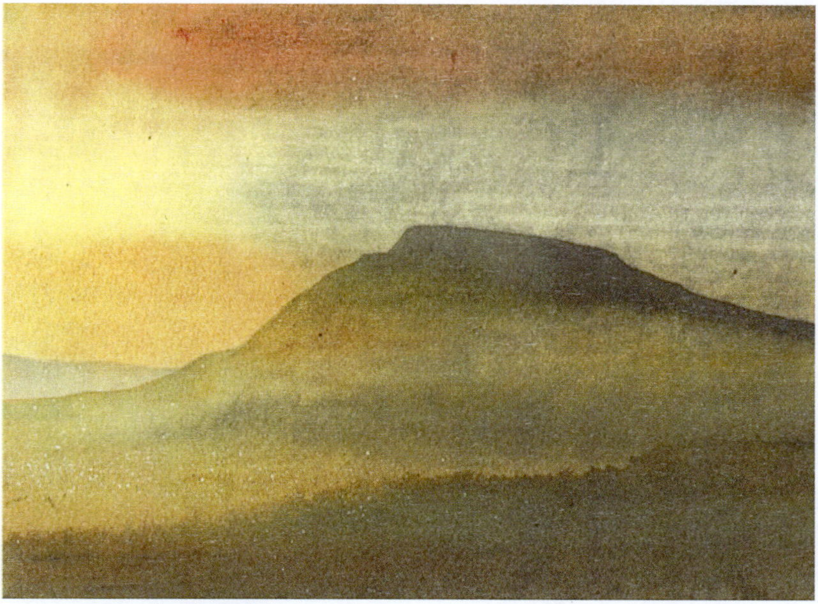

Ingleborough, Evening

The Witch of Clapham that never was

In 1898 a book appeared by R. B. Cragg entitled *Legendary Rambles: Ingleton and Lonsdale*. The text contains a story – a really good story – about the witch of Clapham. It goes something like this:

In the 15th Century a lady named Alice Kettle lived in a cottage near Clapdale Castle, where her foster son, Sir John de Clapham, was the lord of the manor. He was asked to raise a force of five hundred knights to take his part on the Lancastrian side in the Wars of the Roses. Unable to do so he spoke to Alice who was a powerful witch.

She called to the Devil who furnished her with a familiar by the name of Robin Artisson who, under certain conditions, would grant her bidding. The conditions were that she had to sweep the dust on Clapham bridge towards the castle between compline (the last mass of the day) and curfew. As she swept she had to say :

"Into the house of John, my sonne, Hie all the wealth of Clapham town"

At midnight she then had to put nine dead red cockerels in a circle around her on the bridge and call out three times to the familiar.

A few days later a troop of knights rode up the castle, and then more and more until five hundred finally rode away with Sir John to battle in far away Banbury, after which they mysteriously vanished.

Although Sir John triumphed in that battle he was eventually beheaded and, as the story of the knights spread, Alice was taken prisoner and tried for witchcraft. She got off with a light sentence – reroofing Clapham church with lead.

The above story was, not surprisingly, well liked in Clapham – it's a tale with everything – and was retold and reprinted many time, most recently by the local vicar in 1983. Unfortunately it was a tale with a double. The same story occurs at Kilkenny in Ireland.

Mr. Cragg, it eventually turned out, had found the story in an 1843 Camden Society translation from the Irish original that had written in Latin. Obviously short on stories, or hard pressed for time to research , he included the legend in his 1905 book. The truth was discovered by the North Craven Heritage Trust in 2006.

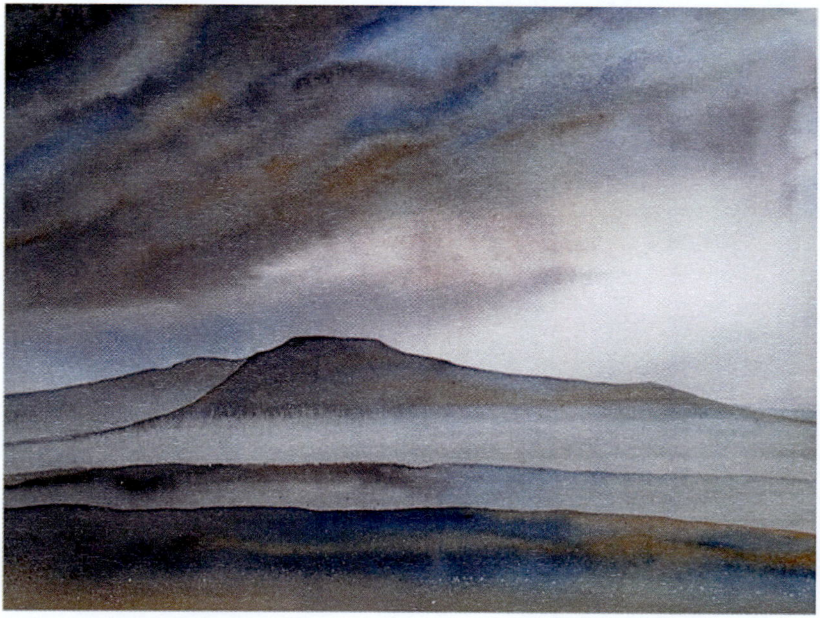

Ingleborough

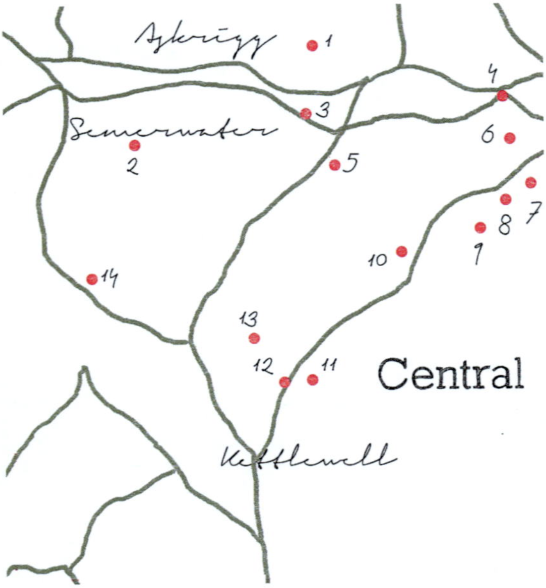

1 Mary, Queen of Scots and Bolton Castle
2 Semerwater
3 Garibaldi's Shirts
4 Wensley
5 West Burton
6 The Penhill Giant
7 The Black Shawl of Coverham & Coverham Abbey
8 The Hermit of St Simon's Chapel
9 The Jacobite of Coverdale
10 Coverdale
11 Lost in the Night
12 Tor Dyke
13 Buckden Pike Memorial
14 Langstrothdale Chase

Mary, Queen of Scots and Bolton Castle

As a son of Scots I grew up with a lot of great stories but few were as terrible as the tale of Mary Queen of Scots. Born of a Royal bloodline, intelligent and beautiful, she should have had it all but she was doomed, She was proclaimed Queen of Scots at six days old. She married a prince of France, became a queen consort of that country but was widowed before the age of eighteen.

Returning to Scotland she married her cousin, Lord Darnley. However her husband was jealous of her friendship with her secretary David Rizzio and organized a conspiracy to murder him. The conspirators, accompanied by a body of armed thugs, carried out the killing in front of Mary (who was seven months pregnant with James VI at the time) after she was forced to hand over Rizzio at gunpoint. They stabbed the Italian courtier fifty-six times. The conspirators were funded by several persons who wished to destabilise Scotland and included Elizabeth I of England, who also provided the conspirators with sanctuary.

Soon after Darnley was murdered in a massive explosion and then things went from bad to worse when Mary married the man accused of Darnley's murder. As public support for her collapsed in Scotland Mary looked for mercy and protection to Elizabeth and England: the last in a long line of bad decisions.

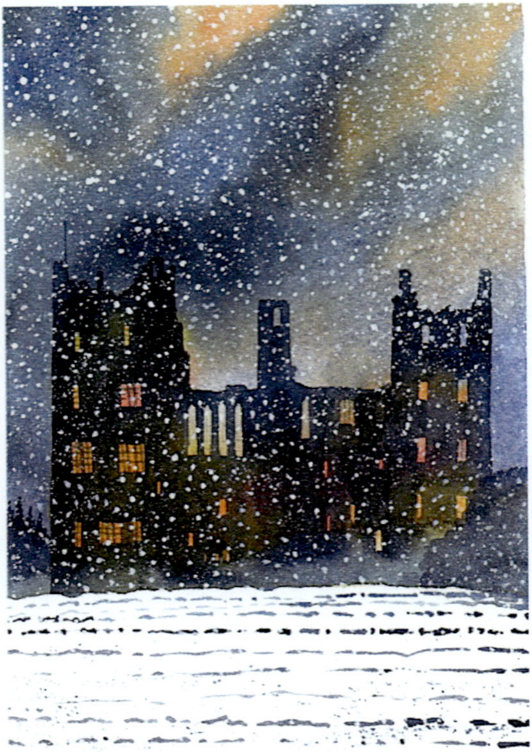

Bolton Castle, Winter

Initially described as a guest, Mary was politically too important to be left at liberty and she became a captive of the English queen, ending up at Bolton Castle in Wensleydale. She was given many of the trappings of a queen: a chamber in the south-west tower, and fifty-one attendants including a secretary, a master of horse and three laundresses. She was also allowed, under tight supervision, to join the hunt. She used this opportunity to gain knowledge of the area so that, if the chance came to run, at least she would know which direction to take.

One day, with the help of a servant, she managed to escape from the castle and made for the nearest town - Leyburn. She took the east lane out of Castle Bolton and made her way to

Warren Wood, at which point she would have been able to hear the hue and cry closing on her. At last she came to the long ridge west of Leyburn and the tale has it that the brambles tore her shawl from her shoulders. She was captured at what has come to be known as Queen's Gap, and the ridge has become known as The Shawl.

Mary was never free again and, before her beheading at Fotheringhay asked her executioner to "make an end of all my troubles". Fearing she might be made a martyr, anything her blood touched was burned including her clothes and the execution block.

Bolton Castle has a chill about it, far beyond the natural coldness of the limestone walls. It's a foursquare stronghold with an air about it unrelieved by the gorgeous countryside in which it sits. It was "slighted"[1] after being surrendered at the end of a siege on November 5th 1645 when the horses had all been eaten.

[1]Partly pulled down to prevent its use as a defensive castle.

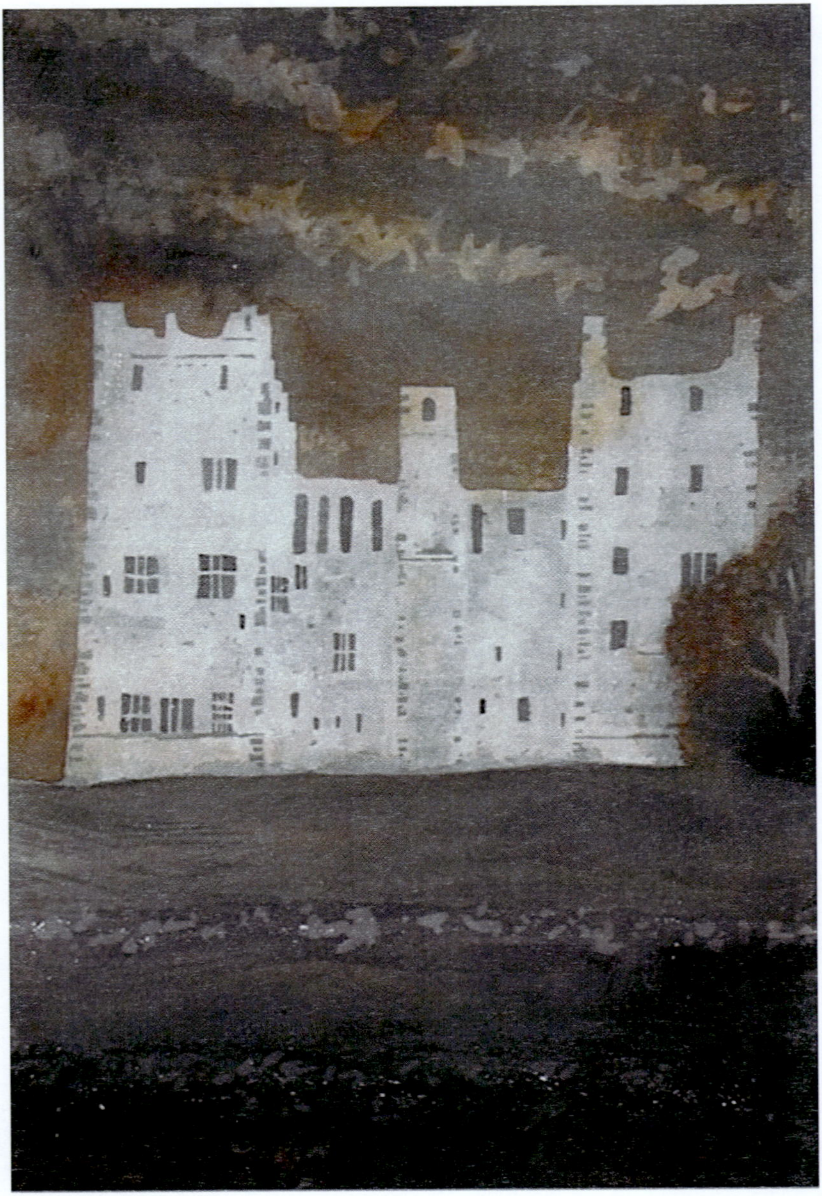

Bolton Castle

Semerwater

The lake of Semerwater lies in a cradle of the hills above Bainbridge. From here flows England's shortest river, the Bain. At the end of the lake are three stones: the Carlow Stone, which was thrown by a giant on Addleborough at the Devil (who was standing on Crag Hill), and the Mermaid Stones which appear to rise and sink. There is some debate about the origins of these stones and cynical scientists have suggested that they may have been placed here by glacial movement, and even that the lake may have been the result of a glacier melting. But this is the true story of Semerwater:

One day an old beggar passed through the city that now lies under the waves. He asked at every house for food and drink, from the humblest hovel to the highest palace, but was turned away. Walking out of the city he came to a shepherd's cottage high on the hillside where he was welcomed in, given cheese, ale and backstone cakes (a kind of Dales oatcake) and a bed for the night.

In the morning the beggar stood at the cottage door and looked down at the city in the valley bottom. He muttered these words:

"*Semerwater rise, and Semerwater sink,*
And swallow the town all save this house,
Where they gave me food and drink."

At once waters began pouring into the valley from the surrounding hills until the city was drowned and every dwelling beneath the water, save for the shepherd's cottage. And this is why, if you take a boat out onto Semerwater and listen in the quiet of the evening, you can hear faintly, from the beneath the water, the church bells rolling and tolling in the slow currents below the surface of the lake.

Since 1956 the old town has had its own annual service on the last Sunday in August when the vicar preaches from a boat.

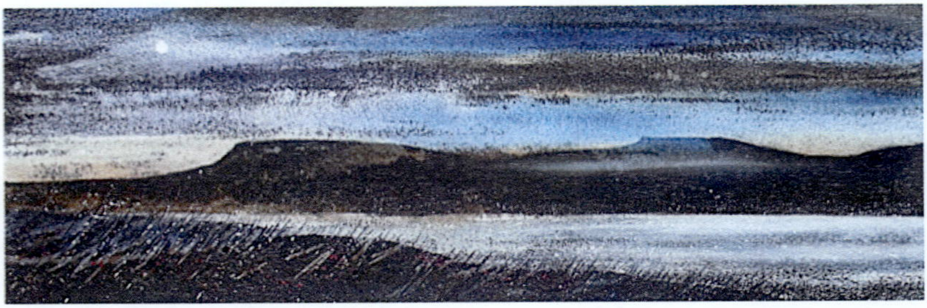
Semerwater by Moonlight

Garibaldi's Shirts

When you come to Yore Mill at the first thing that strikes you is its size. Here is a four storey mill dating from 1784 (with a rebuild in 1870) which would not look out of place in any of the industrial towns of West Yorkshire. It sits by a former packhorse bridge that crosses the River Ure where the three steps of Aysgarth Falls tumble down.

Over the years the building has been a cotton mill, a corn mill, a carriage museum and a chocolate factory but the strangest story attached to this building concerns the general and politician and so-called saviour of modern Italy, Giuseppe Garibaldi.

The story goes that when Aysgarth was producing worsted yarn it was distributed to knitters in the Dale for making into jerseys and socks. When machine-made garments began to appear a stockpile of seven thousand potentially unsalable hand made jerseys was sitting on the mill shelves. In a burst of commercial brilliance, however, the mill owner had the garments dyed red and sold them to Garibaldi to clothe his troops.

There are a couple of problems with this yarn – if you'll pardon the pun. Worsted is usually used to produce a cloth for suits and other tailored garments rather than being knitted into jumpers or socks. Also, in paintings of the great Italian he is definitely wearing a shirt – not a jersey. And the idea that he would come shopping at a Yorkshire mill seems, to say the least, odd, particularly when you factor in the work he had to do: unifying Italy and inventing dead-fly biscuits. However the legend persists and, who knows, it may be true.

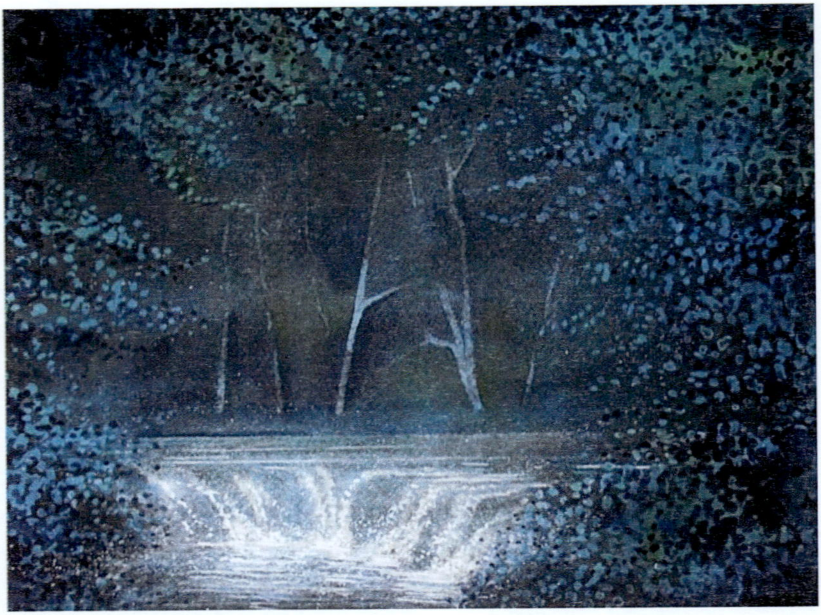
The Upper Falls, Aysgarth

A little way up the hill from Aysgarth Mill is the church of St. Andrew – a 13th Century church "heavily restored" with a full compliment of architectural bells and whistles by the Victorians. The star attraction of the church is the rood screen that came from Jervaulx Abbey. It is a sublime example of sculptural wizardry by the Ripon School of carvers. Thought to date from about 1500 during the tenure of Abbott William de Heslington (who ran Jervaulx from 1472) the screen is a colourful riot of fan vaulting, dragons, antelopes and bizarre fruit. Its all thought to be an allegory on the wickedness of the world - the wages of sin, the demon drink, the beast within and so on – which would have been read like a book by the illiterate 16th Century peasantry.

The screen was saved by twenty Aysgarth men who, just before the abbey was destroyed, walked to Jervaulx and returned with to install their treasure in the church.

Now if you can just drag your tired legs to the top of the hill you come to the Aysgarth Falls Hotel. This was, until recently, the Palmer Flatt Hotel, and stands on the site of a medieval hospice run by the Knights Templars.

The Templars were an elite fighting force in the crusades. They also worked as bodyguards for pilgrims to the Holy Land, developed a banking empire and became immensely wealthy. (A palmer was a pilgrim who had been to Jerusalem and carried a palm leaf as a badge of proof.)

The Knights also had a chapel nearby on the old monastic route of Morpeth Gate. The low walls of the ruin enclose some of the smallest stone coffins you will ever see giving rise to a legend that the Knights would break the bones of the dead to fit them into their tombs. They also ran a Poor House at Ellingstring – poor in the sense of "poorly" – probably for those returning from Palestine with leprosy. The cellars can still be seen in the ruins on the moor there.

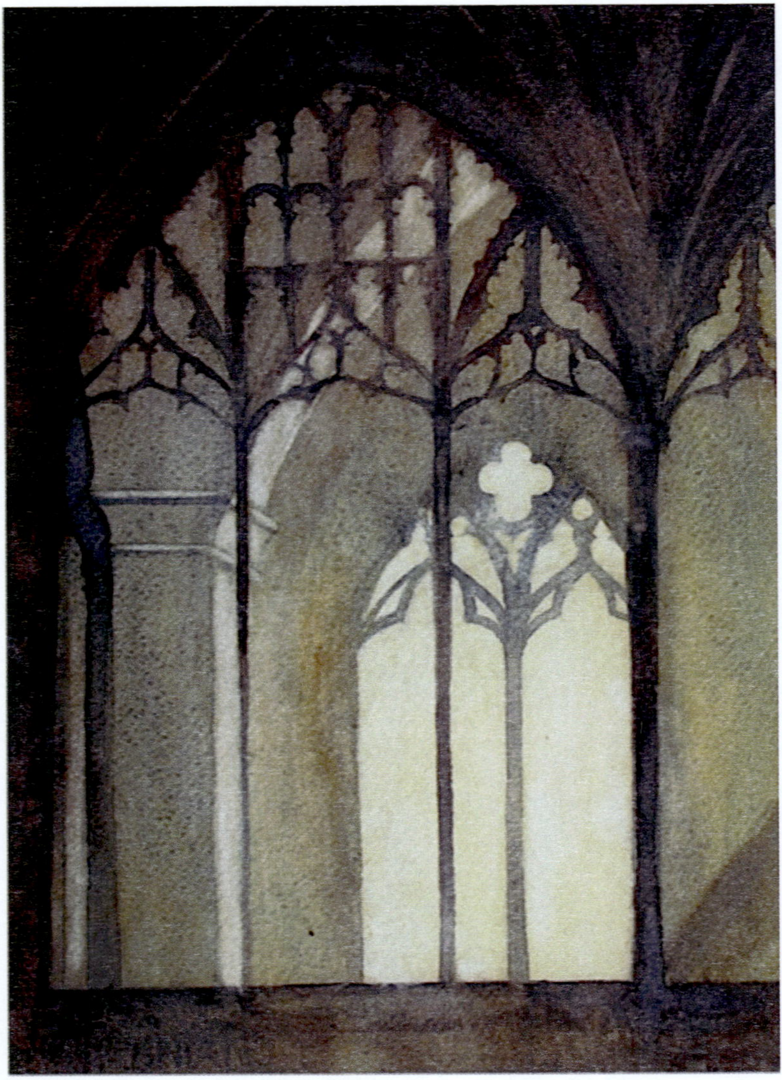

The Jervaulx Screen, Aysgarth

Wensley

There are places that act like magnets for stories and Holy Trinity Church, Wensley, is one of these. Take the building itself. Its mostly 13th century but its standing on the foundations of an 8th century Saxon church. A lot of stones from this earlier church are built into the walls. One gravestone of note is the large blue stone in the main aisle marking where two vicars – a father and son both named Jacob Costabodie – lie buried. It is a local tradition that marriages are carried out on the stone and here is where coffins rest for the funeral service. The chancel, nave, porches, windows and the stages of the tower are all from different periods, but the whole thing is beautifully harmonious.

The outside is known to millions who watched the television series *All Creatures Great and Small* – this was where James Herriot was married in the programme. The churchyard is also the resting place of the comedian Al Read. It is strange to see his worn, crumbling stone and then listen to him sounding fresh as a daisy in his show that is still being repeated on Radio 4.

Inside it's a treasure trove. The most obvious and gorgeously over-the-top piece of furniture is the pew of the Lords of Bolton Castle. It looks like – and many think it is – a box from the Haymarket[1] Theatre in London. The story behind it is this:

Lavinia Fenton played Polly Peacham in the first, massively successful, run of John Gay's *The Beggar's Opera* – one of the biggest smash hits of all time. (So successful that it is still regularly performed, and spawned a musical version by Brecht and Weill called *The Threepenny Opera* that gave the world the song *Mack The Knife*). Back to Polly – this was in 1728. Her number one fan was Charles Bolton, 3rd Duke of Bolton, who fell in love with her from his private box. She became his mistress and eventually his wife, bearing him three sons. There is a lovely piece of documentary evidence: Hogarth's painting of the show portrays Lavinia on stage and Charles watching her from the side of the stage.

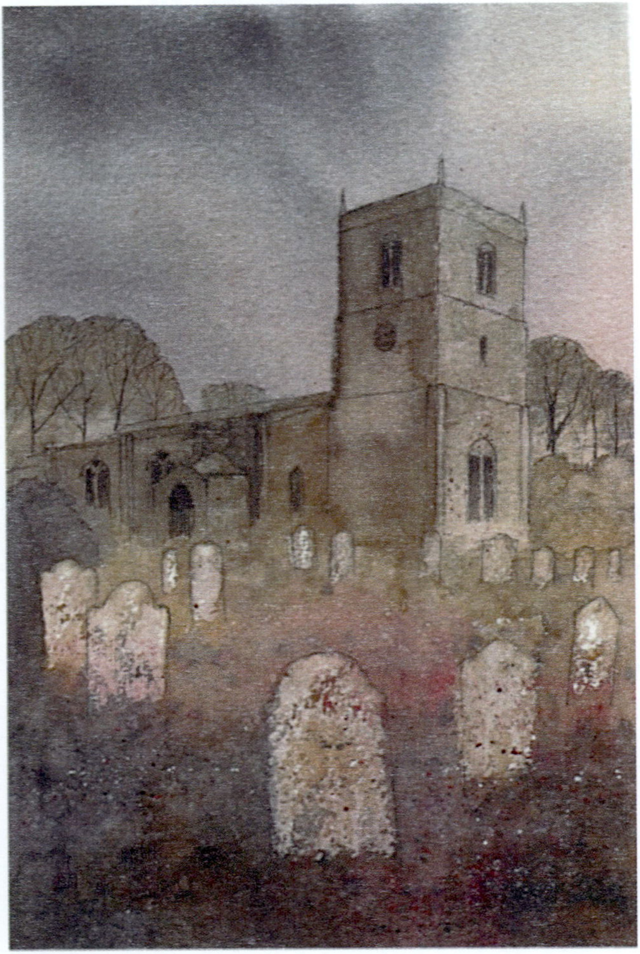

Wensley Church

A slight diversion: Just across the river from the church is a tower on a hill – Polly Peacham's tower. The stories are divided as to whether this was built for her to watch her beloved hunting, or whether it was somewhere she went, out of earshot, when she fancied a warble.

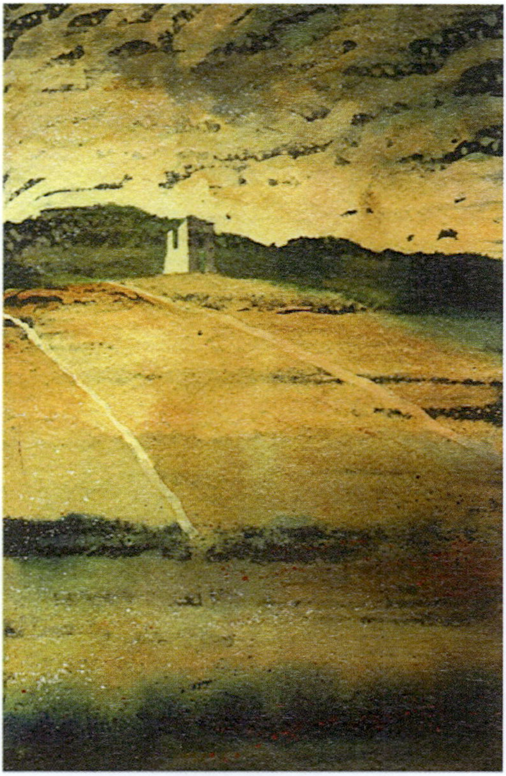

Polly Peacham's Tower

Back in the church, another point of interest is just behind the flamboyant box: part of a medieval rood screen. When Easby Abbey was destroyed in the Dissolution of the Monasteries this screen, from the chantry chapel, was brought here. Possibly more remarkable is what looks like an old offerings box. This is reputed to be the reliquary of Saint Agatha, also from the abbey. (A reliquary was a container for either part of a saint's body or for an object touched by, or associated with them. They're known as first, second or third class relics.) This may have held – may still hold – part of Saint Agatha.

Its one of those churches with everything, including medieval glass and wall paintings. There's also a nice touch on the font cover – a carving of a pineapple dating from 1662. This was a Caribbean symbol of welcome and hospitality which spread to England. Ships captains returning from voyages would put a pineapple on a spike outside their houses to show they were home and that visitors were welcome. Quite a nice idea to put one where babies were welcomed into the church.

[1]Although some say Drury Lane Theatre.

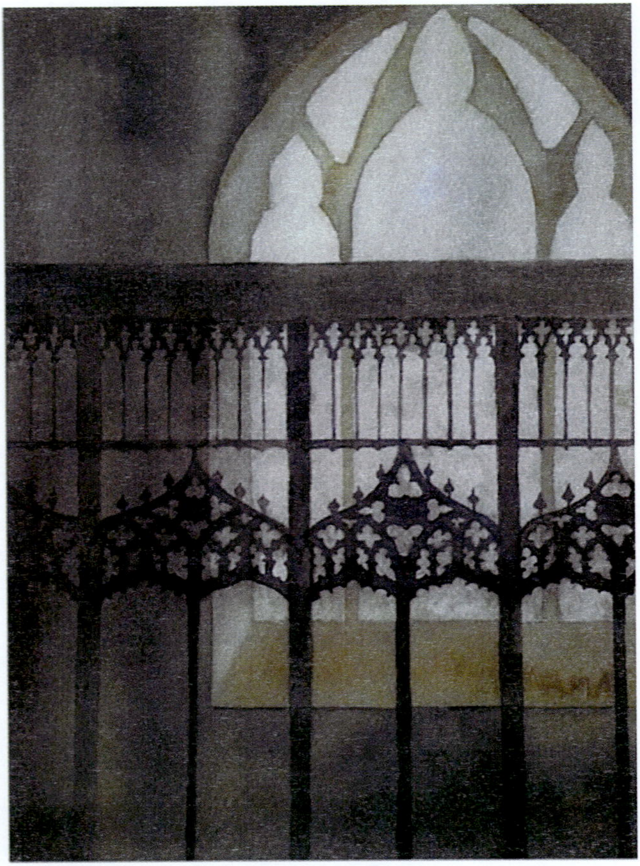

The Easby Screen, Wensley Church

West Burton

JMW Turner, the great English artist, was very fond of the Yorkshire Dales. For fourteen summers he travelled to Yorkshire and sketched everywhere. The sketchbooks are now in the collection of Tate Britain. By leafing through his drawings you can reconstruct the routes he took.

On 27th July 1816 he had stayed at the Green Dragon Inn at Hardraw, and had drawn the wonderful, high waterfall that you reach by the path from the pub's back door. Now Hardraw is impressive and he probably thought he'd seen the best fall in Wensleydale but on the 28th he travelled to West Burton.

If you were trying to describe Cauldron Falls (to give them their correct name) at West Burton, then "perfect" would be pretty close. A falling fan of water cascades over a broad, high rim of rock into a deep circular pool. Trees overhang, reflected in the water where brown trout rise to the fly and crayfish scuttle under stones. The river runs around the end of a ruined mill dam to make a second fall under a packhorse bridge.

West Burton is at the entrance to Waldendale – the Dale of the Welsh, of the Celts – and, approaching it from the main Wensleydale road, you become aware of a slight oddness about the place. There are three follies close to the road: The Rocket Ship, The Gate and The Pepper Pot. The Rocket Ship was built as a cone shaped limekiln but the builder had doubts about its structural integrity and added sloping buttresses which look like the fins on a cartoon spaceship. The Gate is an ornamental arch made of two stone cylinders connected by a curving span – the least impressive of the three. The Pepper Pot is a bizarre construction like a windmill tower built of two storeys with a hole in the top. Its function, apparently, was curing bacon.

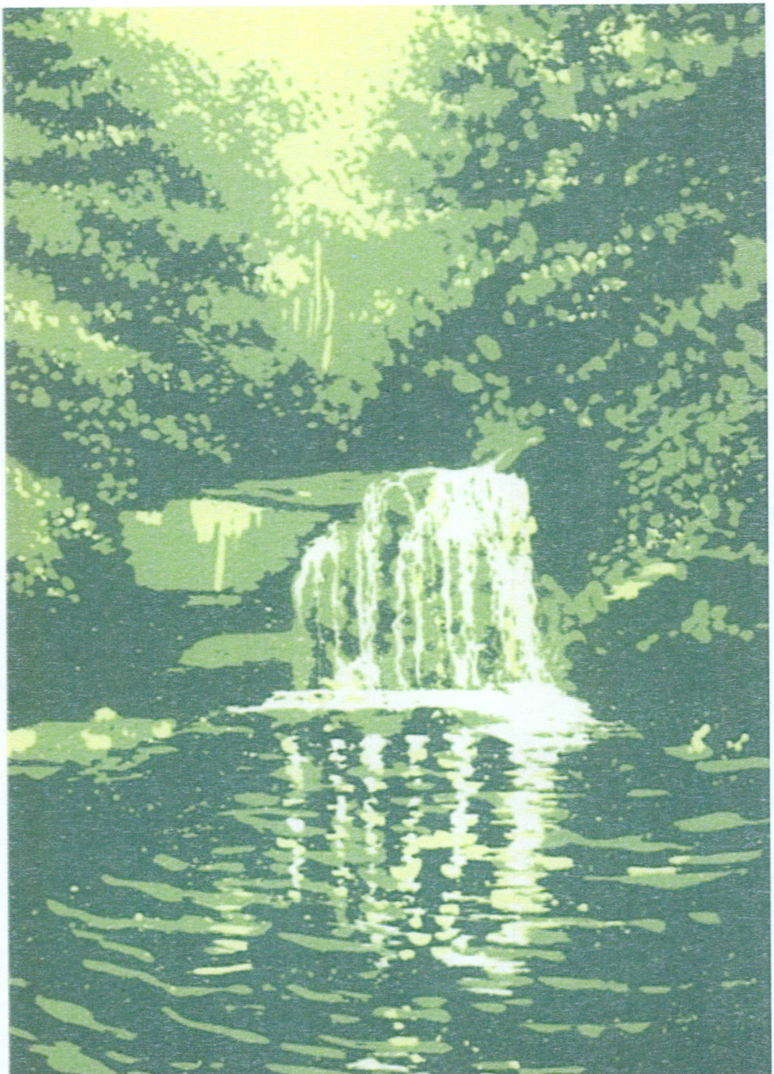

West Burton Falls

The Penhill Giant

Nearly everyone who has travelled through Yorkshire has seen Penhill. If you drive on the A1 there it is on the western skyline. If you're taking the North East mainline, it's away there across the landscape. And, if you're driving into Wensleydale, from the moment you reach East Witton, or come down the hill from Leyburn, you can't miss it.

It's a great hill. Just hard enough to make you feel you've had some exercise, just easy enough for a morning walk. And it's surrounded by history. On the north side is an old monastic track that is marked by a medieval stone cross. On the slopes are worked out bell pits – a sort of early coal mine. And there's an old hollow way which cuts up from Coverdale, crosses the top, and leads down to the packhorse bridge at West Burton.

On the top is a strange, falling down stone shed, a dry-stone pillar with a triangulation point on it and, not far away, a low, stone built, grassy mound which is all that remains of a beacon - one of a series that was built to support a fire to warn England when the Spanish Armada turned up in 1588. Its also known as The Giant's Grave.

The Penhill Giant was very big and notoriously grumpy. He kept a herd of high altitude pigs and a big bad dog with the usual legendary bad dog equipment i.e. teeth like nails, jaws like a steel trap etc.

Occasionally the Giant popped down the hill for a spot of sheep rustling, but he mostly kept himself to himself.

One day a girl was bringing the sheep down from the high moor beside Penhill when one of her flock ran off. With a muttered curse about the intelligence of woolly things she trudged off in pursuit up the hill. Suddenly a cold grey shadow fell over her and when she looked up all she could see was a sky full of giant.

He carried her, kicking and screaming, up the slope and set her down on the hilltop. He was licking his lips as he looked forward to having his wicked way with her, when his (up till now) faithful hound bit him on the leg. The big bad dog had reconsidered where his loyalties lay and, while he wouldn't say no to a nice slice of half-inched mutton, he drew the line at allowing his master to ravish virgins.

The dog chased the giant round and round the hilltop nipping at heels and buttocks until the giant tripped over a boulder and pitched headfirst over Penhill Crags. There was a nasty crunching sound and that was that.

I presume the dog and the maiden lived happily ever after.

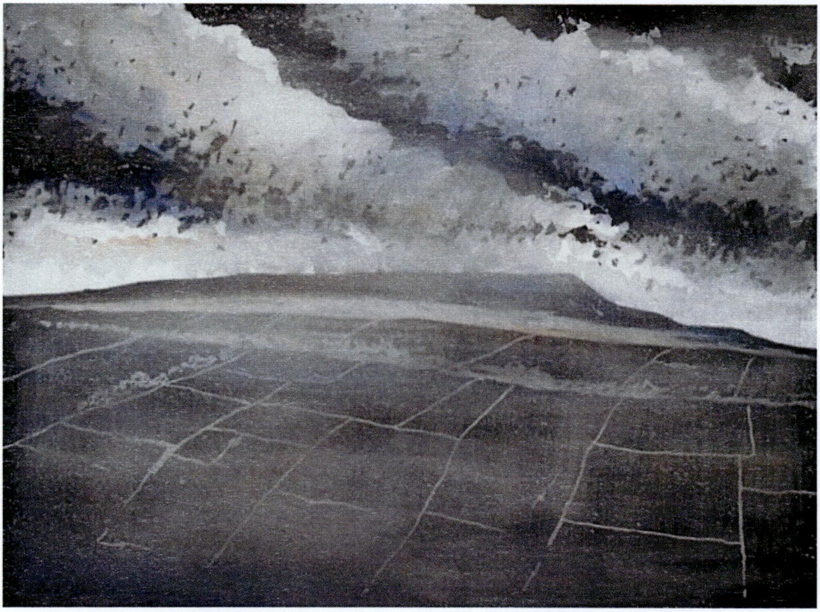

Penhill

The Black Shawl of Coverham

When you come through Middleham you're faced with three great choices. You can carry on through the town and into the heart of Wensleyale, you can stop in Middleham and walk through the ruins of Richard the Third's castle or you can take the road through the town, onto the Low Moor and into Coverdale.

If you take this way you'll probably spend part of it looking at an expensive horse's backside. There are about fourteen stables here training racehorses (they open to the public every Good Friday) and the aristocratic nags seem to spend most of their days clipping and clopping up to the gallops, their jockeys oblivious to the long line of cars forming up behind them.

The road goes over the moor, drops down by Pinkers Pond - a reedy lake in winter and a dried out mudbath in summer – and the most fantastic view opens up as little Coverdale – a mere seventeen miles long – comes into view.

On your left you pass the gates of a big house – Cotescue Park – and then, over the fields, you see Coverham Church - small, grey and lovely. For somewhere with a sad ghost it has a surprisingly happy atmosphere, and there's usually a few sheep cropping the graveyard grass.

If you've timed your journey right you might pass a woman in a black shawl walking from the churchyard, where she spends most of her time lying in her grave. She is making for the gates of Cotescue Park to wait for her long-dead lover.

She was thought to be no more than a figment of rural imagination until a few years ago, when some turf cutters unearthed a corpse in a shallow grave on the moor. What caught their attention particularly – apart from the fact that they were looking at a dead body rather than the usual lump of peat – was that the corpse was wrapped in a black lace shawl.

The story had been around in the Dale for a couple of hundred years, how a poor but beautiful girl, who wore a black lace shawl, had fallen in love with the son of the squire and met him on many a dark night while their respective parents slept. One dreadful day, however, another girl who also fancied the job of Mrs Future Squire put a spanner in the works and told the lad that his girlfriend was playing footsie with someone else.

Overcome with jealousy and rage he waited for his lover that night, blunt instrument in hand, and did her in, before hauling her still-warm body up to the moor and dumping it in a shallow grave.

When she eventually came out of the ground she was reburied at Coverham but, when the time is right, still rises from the grave to seek her lover.

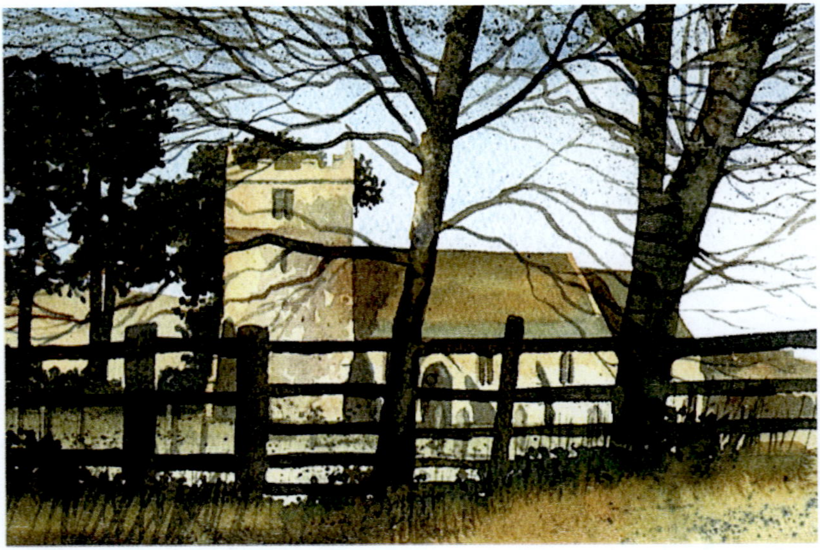

Coverham Church

Coverham Abbey

Coverham Abbey was founded in 1190 at Swainby by Helewise, the daughter of the Lord Chief Justice. She was buried there and, when the abbey relocated to Coverham, her bones were moved to the new abbey's chapter house in 1212.

However, there is little to be seen of Coverham Abbey now. The abbey was largely used as a quarry after the Dissolution to provide stone for the house that now stands there and the grounds are not open to the public. A little bit of the gatehouse has survived and a couple of stone effigies but this place was pretty much deliberately trashed (like Jervaulx) because of its connections. The Neville family of Middleham, who did so much to promote the Yorkist kings were responsible for the abbey's relocation and many of the family were buried here. The Nevilles had contrived to keep the Tudors out of power, and been involved in the Pilgrimage of Grace (Coverham had been one of places for assembling the 30,000 strong army for the cause) against Henry VIII's religious reforms.

Undaunted by Henry's actions, which included beheading Sir Edward Neville, the family rebelled again in support of Mary Queen of Scots in the Rising of the North.

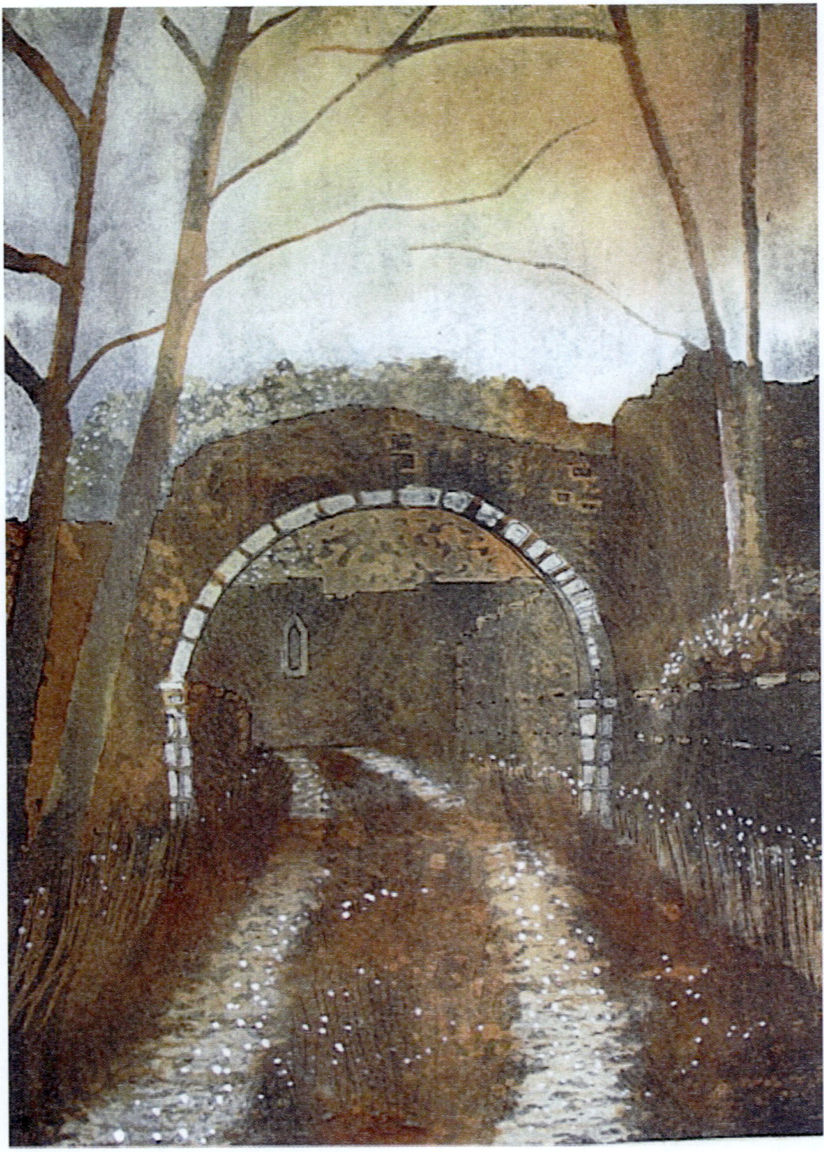

Coverham Abbey

The Hermit of St Simon's Chapel

From the road that runs from Coverham Bridge to Caldbergh a footpath sign directs you down the hill towards the river. As the footpath curves to the left it leads to an enormous limekiln. The circular kiln, which is carved with the date 1786, is one of many in the Dales. They made slaked lime that "sweetened" the soil by reducing its acidity.

On the level ground by the River Cover is St. Simon's Chapel (originally the Chapel of saints Simon and Jude). The ragged walls are all that remains of this chapel-of-ease. Built by Ranulph Pigot (a local lord) in 1328, the chapel was used by those for whom the journey to the church at Coverham was too great. The priest was also required to say mass for the soul of Mr. Pigot. It was, for a while, a hermitage with a resident hermit appointed by Coverham Abbey, and then, in the late 16th century, was in use as an ale house.

It stands now, open to the skies, in this dark, green secret spot. Old tracks lead away, on both sides of the river, from the ford – St Simon's Wath[1] - and you feel perfectly enclosed by the steep valley slopes and the high canopy of thick leaves from overhanging trees.

[1]"Wath" is a word for a ford. It crops up throughout North Yorkshire.

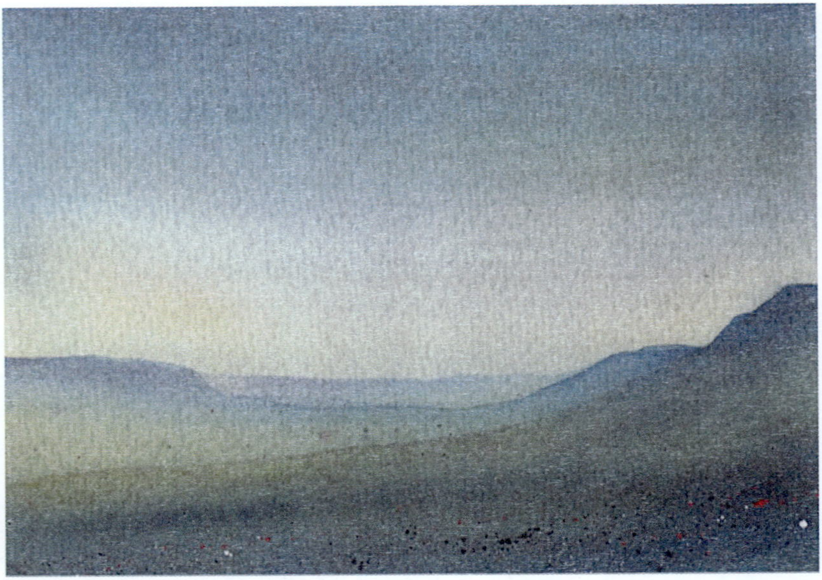

Coverdale, evening

The Jacobite of Coverdale

Coverdale feels like a secret place. It is steep sided and every road but one that leads into it starts high and eventually leads you down into the tight floor of the valley and the graceful Coverham bridge. There is a story that a farm here became home to a man on the run, a story for which the given proof was the existence of a family with ginger hair – the only one in the Dale.

Late in December 1745 the army that Bonnie Prince Charlie had raised in Scotland had marched its way south through Carlisle and Manchester to Derby. Charlie was intending to restore a Jacobean king to the throne, in place of what he, and his father, saw as a Hanoverian usurper.

Its hard now to realise what a dreadful upheaval the fifteenth, sixteenth, seventeenth and eighteenth centuries made of life for many people in England and Scotland. Dynastic wars, religious persecution, economic disasters, failed harvests and the little ice age made for a country in which the ruling class were embroiled in a long series of power struggles, for which many paid with their lives, but not as many as the working people who, when not trying to survive when the rain ruined yet another harvest, were being dragooned into armies to fight for a bewildering roll call of causes.

So it was that a young soldier who had been force-marched one mile too many, slipped away from the Jacobite army on its retreat from Derby and set off for home thought the Pennine drove roads, most of which led to Scotland and home. But he never got there. The story tells that he came down the Red Way – the old road, now a muddy track, which follows Birk Gill (the valley of the birch) in Colsterdale (the dale of the colliers), climbs over the pass into Coverdale and runs down beside Ulfer's Gill (the valley of the wolf) to Caldbergh (the village of the cold stone – a big rock up on the moor). And so he came to the farm of a young widow.

A strong pair of hands was hard to come by in those days, what with one war after another bleeding the young blood of the Dales, and he was probably welcome for that reason alone. However the Jacobite's was a religious cause and, since the young man was probably a Roman Catholic, and the Dales were a Catholic stronghold, he may have landed on his feet on religious grounds as well.

The legends runs that the couple produced a large and healthy family and were very happy. Had he chosen to carry on walking, of course, he would probably have gone down in a hail of grapeshot in the bloody heather of Drumossie Moor, or, as its better known, Culloden.

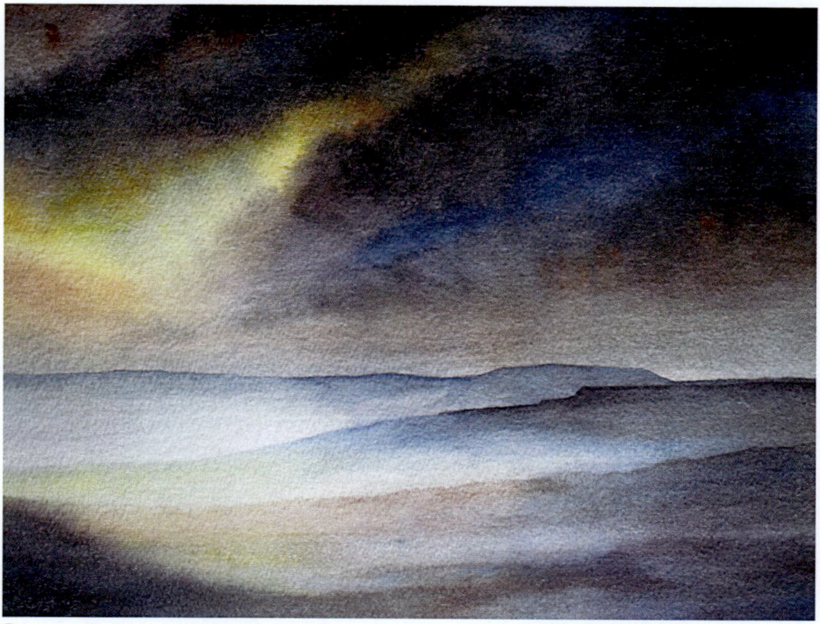
Coverdale

Coverdale

Coverdale is a great place for stories and history. On the south side, just beyond East Witton, is Braithwaite Hall – a 17th century manor house. Up on the hill behind the hall is a fantastically preserved hill fort, one of a number of earthworks in this area. A little further along another hill fort sits on the flank of Crundal Hill: Castle Steads. This overlooks a track that was a communication route during the Civil War and a local story tells of the old fort being used as a gun platform at this time.

A wall runs along the contour line above Castle Steads and here there is a low door in the wall. Through this door is a small valley: the Valley of No Time. From this wrinkle in the hill you are hidden from the world and it is hidden from you. Magical.

A little further, toward Caldbergh, and you can see a large boulder outlined against the horizon. This is the Cold Stone from which Caldbergh takes its name, it was dropped here by a glacier. The climb is steep, but standing on the stone gives an amazing view.

Coverdale was the birthplace both of the first translator of the Bible into English: Miles Coverdale, and Mary Queen of Scot's husband, Lord Darnley.

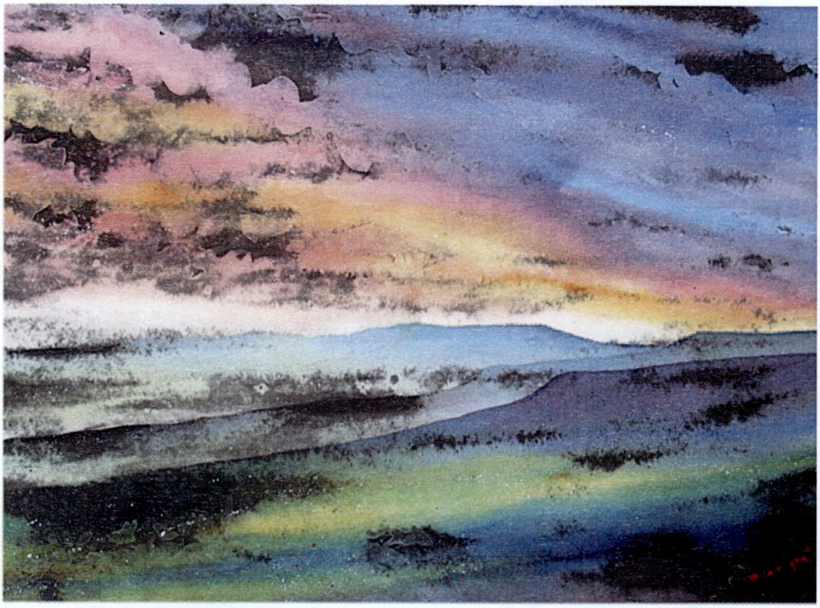

Coverdale from Penhill

Lost in the Night

There are lots of memorials around Yorkshire for aircrew lost during the Second World War. Sometimes there's a small pile of stones on a hillside, sometimes there's a nice cast iron plaque, but sometimes there's just a hole in the ground.

There was a time when the Vale of York was a huge airfield. There were, staggeringly, forty airfields in Yorkshire during the Second World War and eighteen thousand men, mostly shockingly young, died flying from these airfields. Many of them were lost in training flights over the Pennines.

If you take the road from Kettlewell to Middleham and stop at the highest point, Great Whernside lies to the South of the road. A whern, by the way, is an old word for a corn grinding stone and the hard outcrops on the top of the hill have been worked at some time to make these. The view from this hill is one of the most exhilarating in Yorkshire. You can see Nidderdale, Coverdale, Wharfedale and, over the hilltops, the Three Peaks.

On the way up the hill is a crater in the peat, lined with scrap metal, which was made by a very big aircraft. The scrap is actually from three planes which crashed here.

Less than ten miles away at Slipstone Crags in Colsterdale, is a small memorial and some pieces of a plane that crashed on the same night.

The planes were flying from Riccall, near Selby and were crewed by men who were experienced in two-engine planes, but who were being trained to work with four-engine heavy bombers. A training flight was supposed to take them across the Pennines to St Bees Head, along the Scottish border to Hexham, right down the country to Northampton and back to Riccall.

It was a terrible night with high winds, rain and snow storms, and very low temperatures. It was so bad that out of an RAF group of over one hundred and fifty planes in North Yorkshire only the six planes in this flight were in the air. Two of the planes returned to Riccall with icing on their wings that caused one of them to crash. Two others completed the exercise.

At around midnight, about an hour after the planes had taken off, an observer post at Kettlewell reported the sound of a large aircraft "in distress" circling three or four times near Great Whernside in a Force 8 gale. The plane's wings were completely iced over when it made the crater on Great Whernside and the crew of seven died.

At a quarter past one engines were heard near Healey, West of Masham, and, shortly after, a glow appeared at Slipstone crags. The crew of eight also perished.

The awful task of recovering the bodies was performed by conscientious objectors: people who, for moral or religious reasons, refused to bear arms, but were willing to take on non-combat roles such as this appalling work, bomb disposal and fire fighting.

Investigations into the cause of the crash found that the second aircraft had broken up in the air as a result of increased drag caused by a build up of ice, and had hit the ground in a number of pieces.

There seems to be no explanation why, on a night of such dreadful weather, a training flight was sent to fly a circular route over some of England's highest mountains.

There have been dozens of crashes in the Dales and the stories behind them are usually simple cases of bad luck, but these two instances stand out because they were so obviously avoidable.

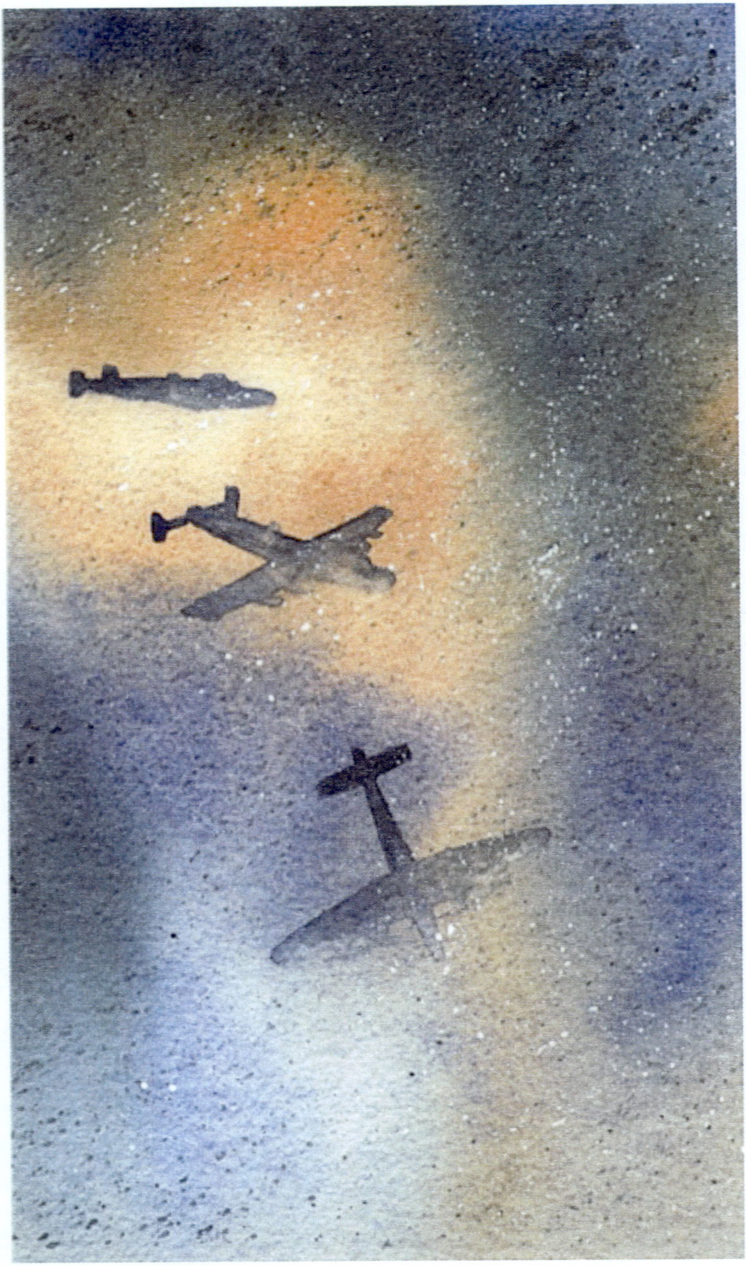

Lost in the Night

Tor Dyke

The road from Kettlewell to Middleham is one of the wonders of the Dales. From the bottom of Wharfedale the road climbs steeply. A track leading off to the left makes towards Cam Head as straight as an arrow – a great walk if your calf muscles are in good condition. Staying on the road you find yourself steadily climbing up a valley with Great Whernside looming up on the right. By a stone built shed there is a pull in. If you stop here, cross the road and hop over the wall at the stile, a path takes you to the entrance of Dow Cave.

This is a cracker. Across a shallow stream, with treacherous slippery stones set with enormous fossils of scallops, a great dark cave mouth beckons you in. It's worth a look inside. Few cave entrances in the Dales are as accessible. This is where cave rescue groups learn their trade. Some way further inside, and only for the well equipped and experienced, are some lovely water carved galleries.

Back on the road you are at the foot of the fearsome Park Rash – a hill that feels close to the vertical. Amazingly stage coaches used to use this route. I dread to think how they managed in winter.

As the road comes to the top of the pass you can see, on either side, a deep ditch, and bank topped with a stone wall – like the defences of a castle. This is Tor Dyke.

Originally thought to be created by Venutius[1] to defend the Brigantes tribe from the Romans in about AD 70 this is now thought to be the border of the Dark-Age Kingdom of Craven.

It is a wonderful place. The views down towards Kettlewell and beyond are terrific. You feel to so high and yet sheltered by the bulk of Great Whernside to the south. From here you can look down on circling birds (and occasional RAF jets). Looking to the East is the length of Coverdale, the hills receding in the blue distance to Penhill and, far away, the line of the hills beyond the Vale of York. In a short walk you can be over Great Whernside and looking down Nidderdale or walking North to Buckden Pike and down into Waldendale. It's the Clapham Junction of the Dales

[1]Venutius is also thought to have been behind the creation of the hillfort on Ingleborough which was enclosed by a wall 3,000 feet long.

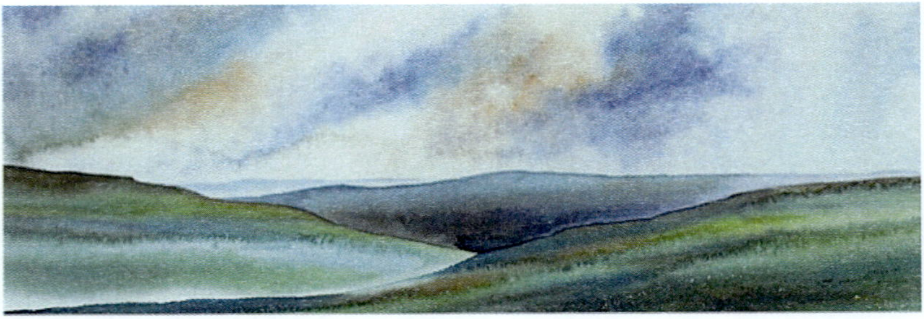

Looking from Tor Dyke

Buckden Pike memorial

On the peaty, boggy summit of Buckden Pike is a stone cross, rising out of a wide base. In the concrete of the base are twisted, corroded pieces of an aeroplane and a bronze fox's head. The old roads, which have been little used since the motorcar came along, cross this hill from Waldendale to Kettlewell, and across the ridge to Great Whernside and down to Coverdale or Nidderdale. Whichever way you approach the summit it's a hard uphill walk, unless you arrive by air.

This memorial, and the story that goes with it, is one of the best known in the Dales, but it's a good enough tale to stand telling a few times.

On a cold winter's morning – the 30th January 1942 – the temperature had dropped like a stone and a strong wind was blowing thick snow against the the six foot dry stone wall on the hill's crest.

Flying through the white sky was a Wellington bomber from Bramcote with a Polish crew. Trying to fix their position, they circled a town without identifying it (it was Skipton) and took the decision to fly north in search of a landmark. Of course this was the worst direction they could have taken, leading them over the highest hills in the Dales.

The plane – flying perilously low - was heard by a number of people, but from the pilot's seat there was nothing to be seen but a wall of white. The rear gunner, Joe Fusniak, later recalled that the pilot had said he was closing the engine cowls to warm the engines but his next sensation was of being violently shaken and battered.

He found himself in deep snow surrounded by the ruins of his gun turret. The plane had disappeared. With a badly wounded leg he set off across the ridge and, several hundred yards away found the wreckage. The plane had hit the top courses of the wall. A couple feet higher and the Wellington would have missed the hill altogether. Of his comrades only one man, terribly injured, was still alive. Joe used a parachute to keep him warm, and left him with a tin of soup – the only sustenance he could find under the circumstances.

Joe realized that neither he, nor his crewmate, would survive if he couldn't get off the hill and find help. He chose a direction at random, and, using a broken spar for support, began to drag himself through the snow. He came across a set of tracks – the footprints of a fox. Reasoning that, in this weather, a fox would be seeking somewhere sheltered, Joe followed the tracks. Had he continued in his original direction he would have headed into the heart of the moors.

At last he reached a dry-stone wall and stopped. Hypothermia was setting in, his could see only visions, and he prayed aloud in desperation. As if in answer, a ray of light burst through the clouds and the valley – Upper Wharfedale - was revealed. He cried out for help and was answered by Nannie Parker – the daughter of the landlord at the White Lion Inn, at Cray.

They carried him into the pub, thinking from he was a German airman. In broken English he made them understand what had happened but, with the worsening weather, a rescue party could not set out till the next day. Unfortunately by the time they found the crash Joe's crewmate had died.

Sergeant Joseph Fusniak was awarded the British Empire Medal by King George VI, and was decorated by Chief Air Marshall Harris. After the war he returned to Cray many times and, on one visit in 1973, built the memorial which now crowns Buckden Pike, expressing his eternal grateful to that fox.

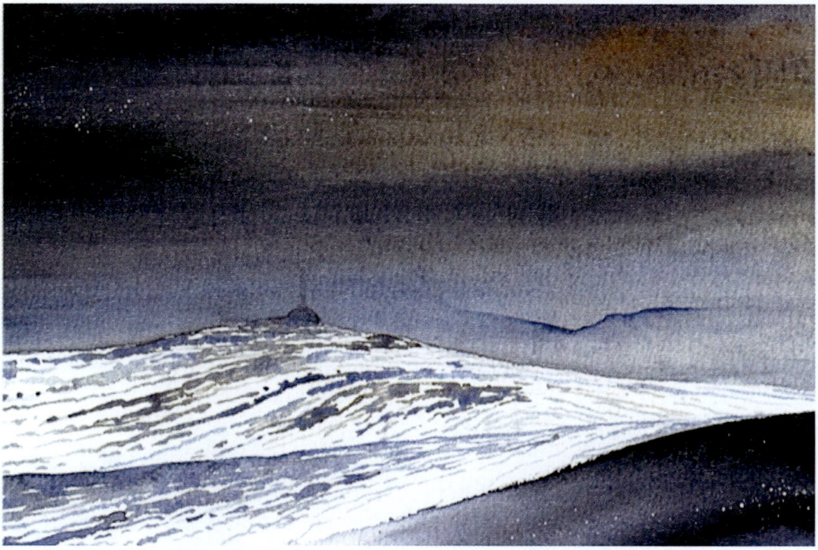

Buckden Pike Memorial

Langstrothdale Chase

There is a dreadful old movie that was made in 1949 - *A Boy, A Girl and a Bike* - which stars a very young Honor Blackman (Pussy Galore in *Goldfinger*). It creaks along with a group of cyclists escaping the mill towns for the Dales. The best things about it are the locations which include Hebden Bridge, Malham and Upper Wharfedale. At one point the riders take a break near a river trickling over a series of broad flat limestone steps. This is Yockenthwaite in Langstrothdale Chase.

If you travel into the Dales via Wharfedale the road seems to go on forever. After Bolton Abbey, the Strid and Barden Tower are left behind, there are Grassington, Kilnsey Crag, Kettlewell and Hubberholme before the Dale turns left and the river becomes "nowt but a bairn".

Hubberholme is tiny – a church and the George Inn. Hubba was a Viking chieftain who settled here in the ninth century. The George has an annual candle auction known as the Hubberholme Parliament. The vicar sits in the House of Lords (the dining room) and the bidders in the House of Commons (the bar). A candle is lit and the bidding begins. Whoever bids last before the candle goes out gets to rent 16 acres of church land.

In the church is a rare surviving rood loft and screen that is reputed to have come from Coverham abbey. These screens must have been of great significance since, as the threat of Henry VIII's destruction of the monasteries became a reality, many of them were "rescued". This gem is the most complete example.

Beyond the church the road rambles up and down before settling by the river. It is perfect paddling country. Across the river is the tiny stone circle of Yockenthwaite. Most of the stones push up no more than a foot or two out of the grass and the diameter of the circle is about twenty-five feet. Stonehenge it isn't. What is more it isn't a stone circle either.

These twenty or so stones are the kerbstones of a burial mound[1] that has completely eroded away. The tomb entrance can vaguely be made out on one side. Who was buried here we can only guess, but its one of the most beautiful spots in the Dales.

[1]There is a similar arrangement of kerbstones known as the Giant's Grave near Halton Gill.

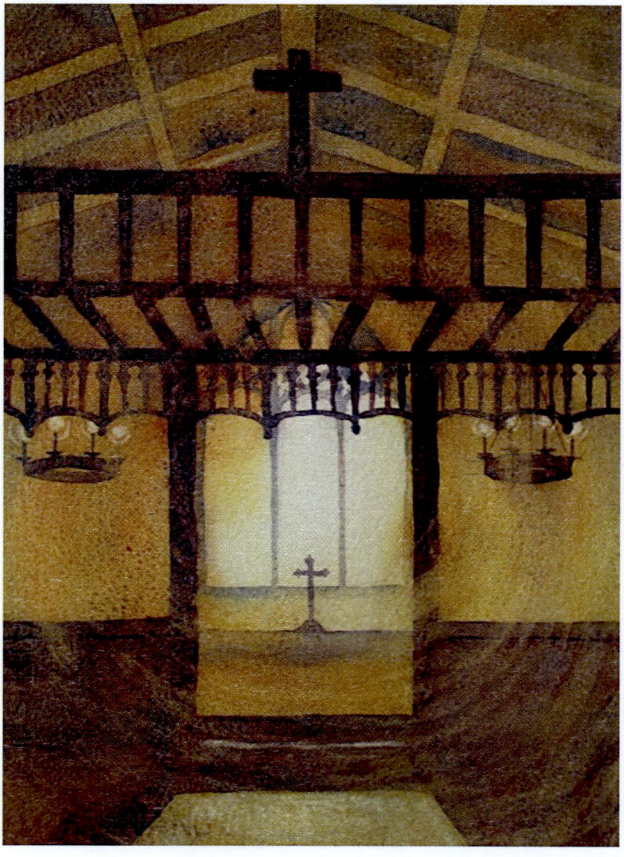

Hubberholme Rood Loft

East

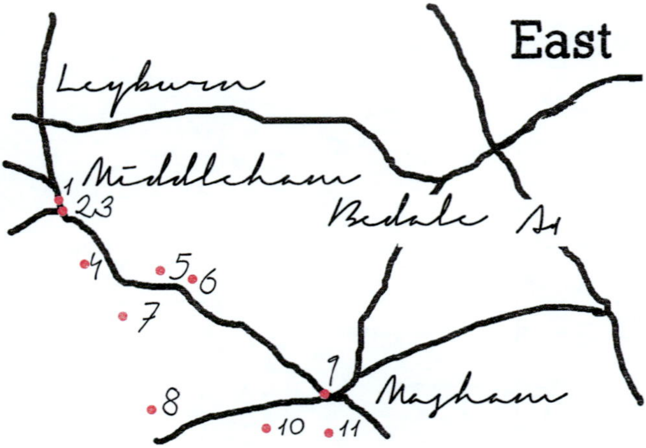

1 Middleham - Castle Bridge
2 St Alkelda's Well
3 The Middleham Jewel
4 Slavering Sal
5 Jervaulx Abbey and the Pilgrimage of Grace
6 Kilgram Bridge
7 The Colsterdale Man of Mystery
8 The Leeds Pals
9 The Masham Bones
10 William Danby & Druid's Temple
11 Nutwith Cote Stables

Middleham Castle Bridge

Just outside Middelham is a bridge that thinks it's a castle. This is actually a very early suspension bridge. If you look at the top of the towers you can see where the cables were attached.

Built in 1830 the bridge worked well for a while until a herd of cattle were either too heavy or set up a destructive vibration by getting into step. Either way the bridge was altered to a more conventional form in 1865.

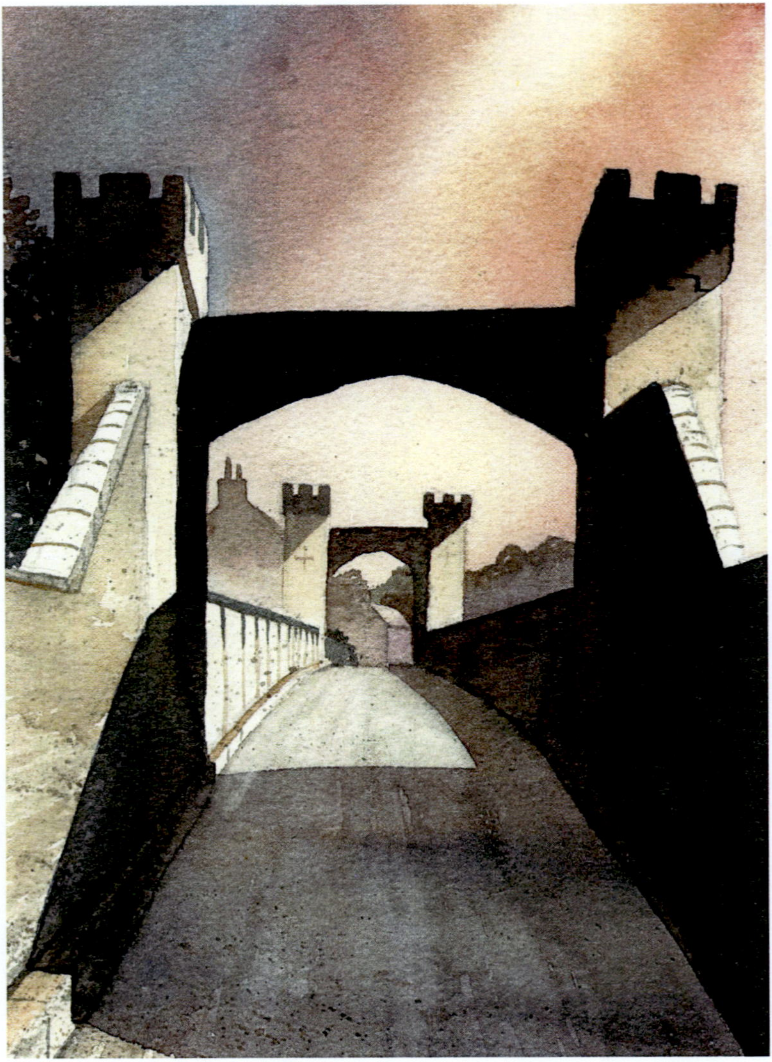

Middleham Castle Bridge

St Alkelda's Well

There is a square hole at the foot of a drystone wall in Middleham. Over the wall is a housing estate and close by is a newish school. Until the school was built, water flowed through here but the building work screwed up the water supply and its been dry ever since. Does it matter? Well, to me, yes, because this is a Holy Well dedicated to St Alkelda who was martyred here about twelve hundred years ago.

The parish church is dedicated to her (and so is one at Giggleswick) and, if you had a problem with your eyes a few hundred years ago this is where you came. You would say a few words, maybe write them on a strip of cloth and tie them to the overhanging trees, dip your hand in the water and, hopefully, you eyesight would improve.

Who was Alkelda? She was either a Saxon princess, a noblewoman or a nun. She was chaste, a devout Christian and was murdered in a horrible fashion.

In the Ninth Century most of the North was being colonised by Scandinavian farmers and their families but, leading this wave were Viking warriors. Some of them were politically astute and found ways to work with local leaders who realised that resistance was futile. The Vikings who came to Middleham were cut from different cloth. As an example to any who might wish to perpetuate the denial of Viking gods an example was made. Alkelda was murdered by two Danish women who used a long strip of cloth wrapped around her throat to strangle the life out of her.

There are holy wells all over England, mostly forgotten, but very few as ill served as this one. Within a few miles of Middleham there are two on East Witton Fell, one which emerges through the wall of Swinton Park and another at Ilton.

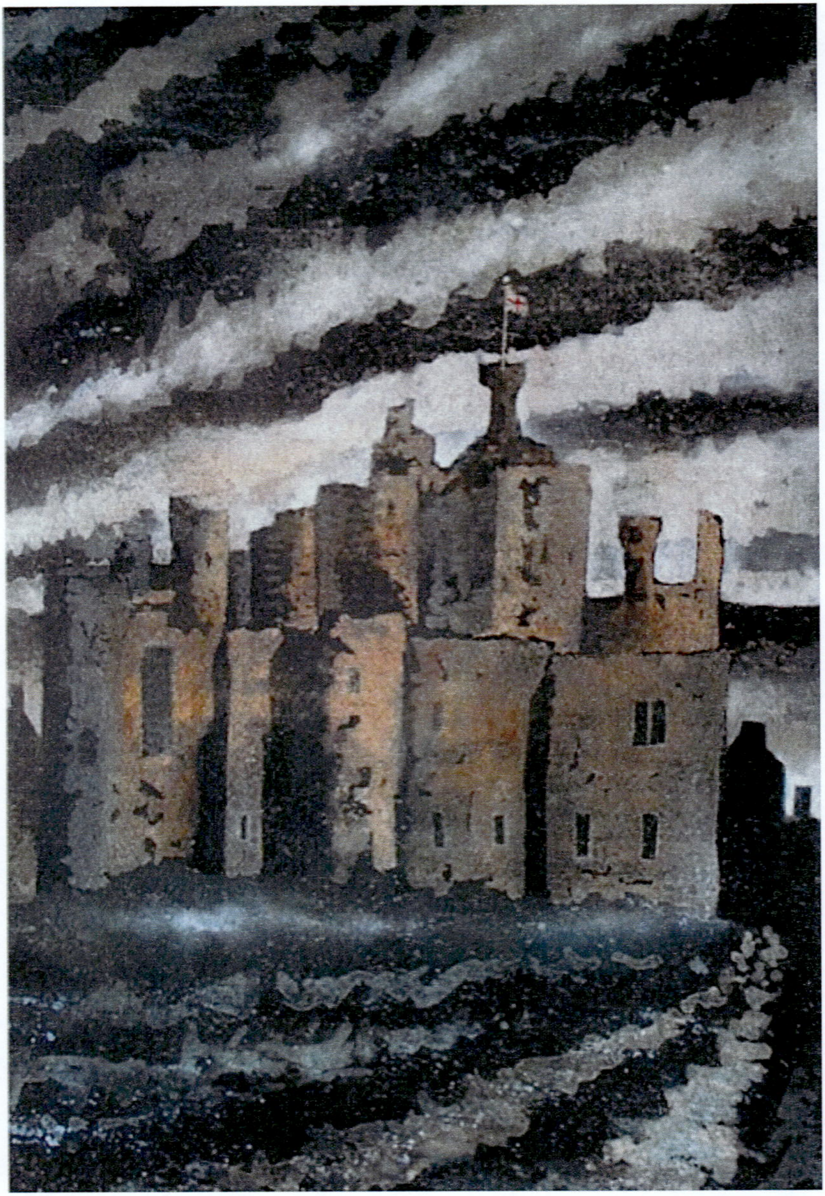

Middleham Castle

The Middleham Jewel

Middleham Castle was known as "the Windsor of the North" in the reign of Richard III: a massive keep rising three stories high surrounded by a bakehouse, brewery, garderobes[1] and living quarters. The whole complex is entered though a gatehouse, complete with murder holes[2]. It used to be an even larger castle but the outer bailey disappeared at some point. The houses in front of the castle were built from its stones.

The first fortress is the earthwork on the hill behind the castle, The climb up William's Hill is well worth the effort: the view is fantastic. There is a local variation on a widespread legend: if you run three times widdershins (that's counter-clockwise) round the earthwork a door will open to reveal lost treasure where you stop.

Between William's Hill and the castle is a sloping field and it is somewhere in this area that Ted Seaton was metal detecting in 1985. He was about to pack up for the day when he got a faint trace of metal. He unearthed what he thought was a powder compact and went home. Only when he started cleaning the object did he realise what he had found: a wonderful piece of Gothic jewellery weighing 68 grams and set with a large, 10 carat sapphire.

The Middleham Jewel is a very beautiful gold pendant, engraved with a depiction of the holy trinity on the front, the nativity on the back and bordered with a prayer or charm to protect the wearer from the "falling sickness" – epilepsy. It was made in a London workshop in the fifteenth century for someone with a lot of money and, presumably, epilepsy. The likely owner could have been any of a number of people – possibly Anne Neville, who grew up at the castle and married Richard the Third (who also grew up here), Richard himself or possibly their son, Edward. Anne died young, at twenty eight. Richard perished on Bosworth field – a king for a mere two years. Edward of Middleham, Prince of Wales, was known here, and at Richard's other castle at Sherriff Hutton, as Lal

Crookback. (Crookback was Richard's nickname, derived from his hunchback – the result of a condition that contorted his spine. "Lal" is an affectionate Yorkshire term for "little"). A sickly child, he was born in Middleham in 1473 (possibly in the castle's Prince's tower), and died 1484.

The jewel is full of medieval meanings. The sapphire is a symbol of the splendour of heaven, based on a reference in Exodus. A quotation from the *Agnus Dei* – part of the Latin mass[3] – ends here with word *Ananizapta* – a symbolic word meaning "Have mercy upon us, O Judge". The combination of the Agnus Dei with an image of the Nativity are symbols which, when taken together, suggest that it was worn by a pregnant woman.

The jewel was ruled not to be treasure trove and was eventually bought by the Yorkshire Museum where it is now on show. The visitor's shop at Middleham Castle has a replica. It is a beautiful window into a world that we only usually see through the gory stories of the Wars of the Roses.

[1] A garderobe is a medieval toilet which emptied its contents into a sump at the foot of the garderobe tower. One of the worst jobs for any castle employee was emptying this out.
[2] A murder hole is an aperture where those guarding a castle can fire arrows or drop stones or - always a classic - boiling oil on attackers. At Middleham invaders could be trapped between two portcullises (portculli?) and disposed of in this way.
[3] O Lamb of God, that takest away the sins of the world, have mercy upon us.
O Lamb of God, that takest away the sins of the world, grant us thy peace.

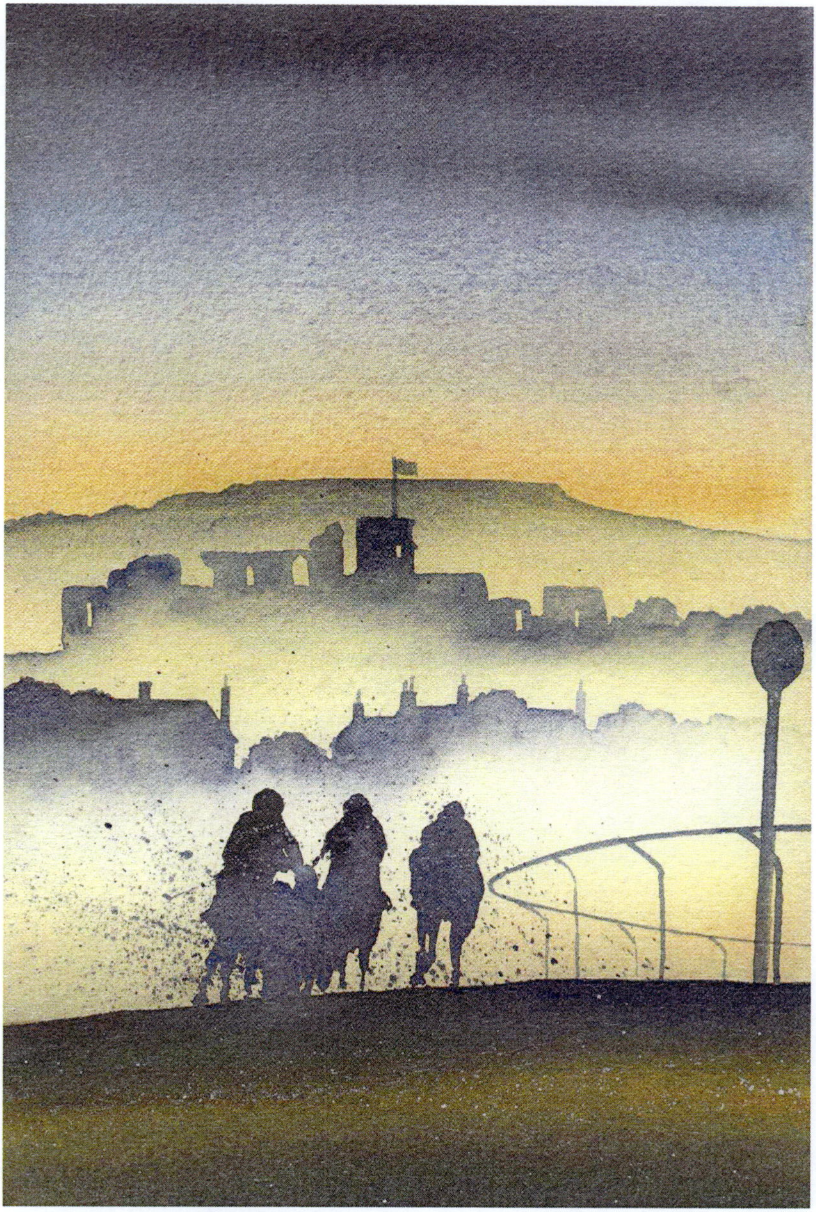

Racehorses on Middleham Moor

Slavering Sal

On East Witton Fell there is a tract of woodland. Across the path is a gate carrying signs with words like PRIVATE and KEEP OUT but, if you risk the wrath of the timber company, you will come to an old, deeply rutted track called Cast Away Ride. The very fact that the track has a name is enough to draw one in to explore, and what does "Cast Away" mean?

The track forks (take the left hand way) and the ground rises. On the left of the track, a small stone grotto comes into view. It has a stone table inside and an amazing view of Wensleydale outside.

This was the favourite picnic spot of the Earl of Aylesbury. He was fond of Wensleydale and, in the eighteenth century, rebuilt the charming village of East Witton, complete with a schoolhouse and a piped water supply – a real rarity at that time. Keen to make the perfect village he built a new church at the head of the village green. He demolished the old one which was perfectly okay, but in the wrong place. He built this little picnic grotto in 1821 and the track is the end of a carriageway he had made from his house.

Set to the left of the grotto is the star attraction: a stone head, known as Slavering Sal, out of which pours a stream of clear water into Cast Away Well - thought to be a Celtic holy well. The practice of casting articles into it for wishes or to pray to some deity gives it its name. It is sometimes known as Diana's Well.

There is a local rhyme associated with Slavering Sal:
"Whoever eats Hammer Nuts and drinks Diana's water
Will never leave Witton town while he has a rag or tatter."

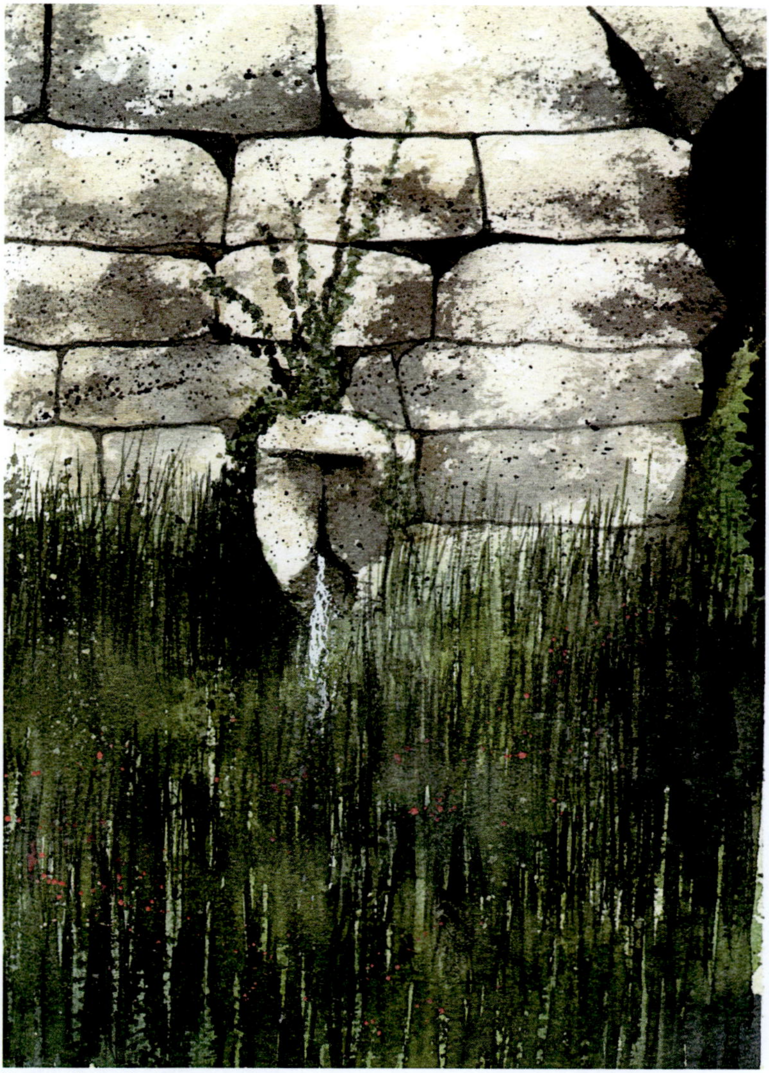

Slavering Sal

Jervaulx Abbey and the Pilgrimage of Grace

For my money Jervaulx is the loveliest of Yorkshire's abbeys. It lacks the grand churches of Fountains and Rievaulx but it also lacks their over-manicured polish. Jervaulx is a ruin that looks like a ruin should – wild flowers grow out of the walls, the grass grows long and the moss grows thick.

The reason why Jervaulx's church was completely destroyed had to do with an event called the Pilgrimage of Grace. This was a northern rebellion to stem Henry VIII's seizure and dissolution of the monasteries. While many houses were closed down, their assets seized and sold and their monks pensioned off, Jervaulx's abbot, Adam Sedbar decided to make a stand. Robert Aske, a lawyer and a cousin of Henry's wife Jane Seymour, became the leader of the rebellion that drew in several other prominent churchmen including abbots from Bridlington and Fountains.

It was decided to make an example of Jervaulx. Sedbar was seized, trying to escape, on Witton Fell. He was taken to London and hanged, drawn and quartered. His head was then spiked on London Bridge. The abbey church – by all accounts a sublime example of Gothic architecture - was set with explosive charges and reduced to rubble.

The abbey has had a lasting effect on life in the Dale however. It was at Jervaulx that Wensleydale cheese was first made, probably from sheep's milk. The distinctive taste of this cheese (made even more famous by Wallace and Gromit) is down to the mixture of herbs which grow in the grass in Wensleydale's upland pastures.

The abbey's other legacy results from the monk's interest in racing horses, and the profusion of racing stables at Middleham are thought to be a direct result of this tradition.

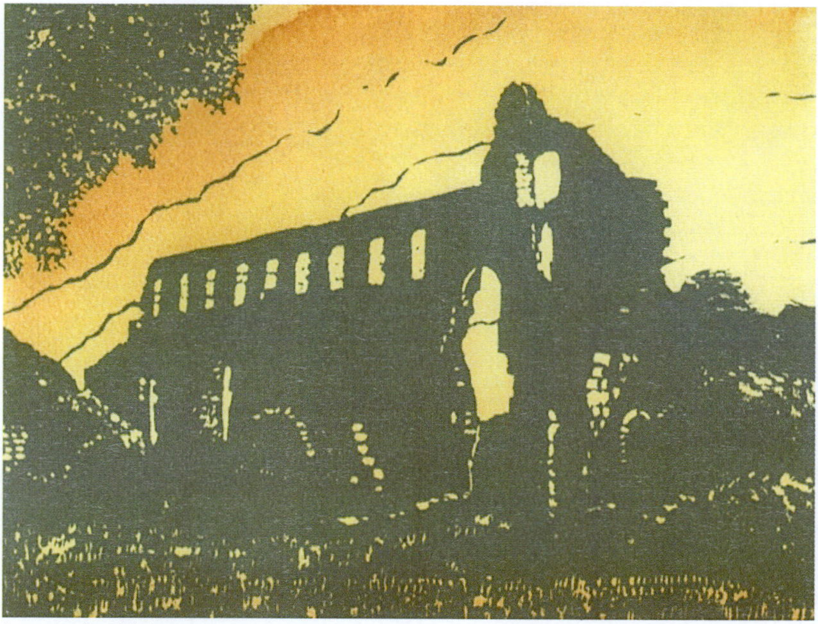

Jervaulx Abbey

Kilgram Bridge

Just downstream from the beautiful ruins of Jervaulx Abbey, is Kilgram Bridge. A solid, six arched construction, this is a remarkable structure with a secret: it is built on a fabulously preserved Roman paved ford, and owes part of its longevity to this firm foundation.

The ford is the crossing point of a Roman road from Ripley to Catterick. Beneath the shallow water is a broad expanse of sandstone blocks held together with white mortar. Its state of preservation is only matched by that of the structure standing on it. Kilgram (AKA Kilgrim, Kelgrimhou or Kylgramhowe) Bridge was built around 1145 by either the monks of Jervaulx Abbey or ... the Devil!

The River Ure has never been a quiet, predictable river. When the rains come to Wensleydale it rises quickly, bursts its banks and sweeps away anything not firmly tied down. So it was that many flimsy wooden bridges were built and lost before the Devil came along.

He offered the locals a bargain: he would build a bridge so strong that it would last many lifetimes BUT – and in this sort of story its usually a big but – in return he would take the life of the first living thing that crossed the bridge. The villagers were so desperate that they accepted his terms and in a single night the bridge was built.

In the morning the Devil appeared to accept payment. A man came forward to cross the bridge – a shepherd whose flock was the other side of the river. He had spent the night thinking and he had a plan, a plan that would demand a heavy personal sacrifice. He stood on the threshold of the bridge but, instead of crossing, leapt the parapet and swam to the other bank. Rising from the water he whistled to his dog. The faithful hound crossed the bridge and the Devil was paid.

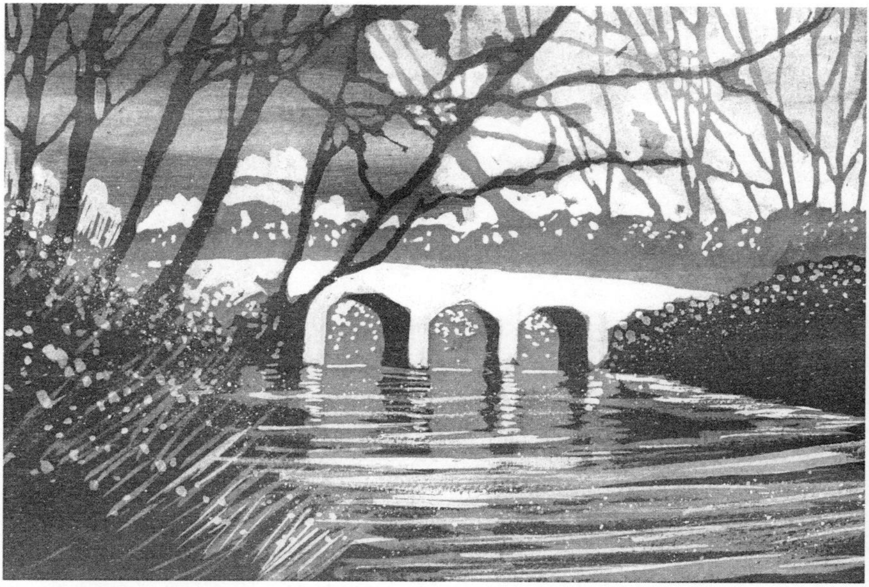

Kilgram Bridge

The Colsterdale Man of Mystery

The Dales are a strange combination of cosy villages, rambling roads that thread through the valleys and bleak empty moorland. Walking the moors is one of my greatest pleasures but the remoteness these open spaces, studded with old coal pits, lime kilns, grouse butts and prehistoric earthworks, is sometimes brought home with a story like this one:

The gamekeeper had noticed traces of bone flecking the peat for about four years as he passed the ditch on Thorny Grange Moor, but he thought they were the remains of a long-dead sheep. When he finally had a closer look. in May, 1997, the grisly truth became apparent. The remains were of a man who would have been about sixty when he died, the time of death being around twenty years earlier, in 1977.

The decased was dressed in a grey suit, a white shirt, a brown and orange tie and a pair of shoes by the George Ward Boot Company. In his pockets he carried a 1958 shilling, a 1971 penny, a mortice key in a tin, and a Cadaux 600 transistor radio. At some time in the distant past he had fractured his left collar bone, two ribs, both heels and suffered from mild arthritis.

Despite all this information, a facial reconstruction and a lot of publicity the Colsterdale Man was never identified. In a very sad press release a spokesman said: "A tooth has been retained for DNA comparisons."

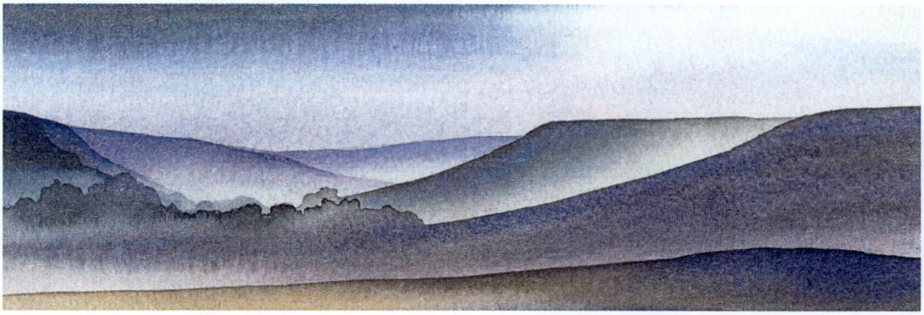

Colsterdale

The Leeds Pals

Among the scores of stories to come out of the First World War, those of the "Pals" battalions are some of the saddest. The concept of recruiting a lot of boys from the same part of the same town, training them together and sending them to fight together had a number of effects. After the war it left gaping holes in many districts where a generation had been wiped out. And the pain of watching your closest friends die around you must have been appalling.

At Breary Banks in Colsterdale Leeds Water Board owned a tract of land that had been a workers camp for building a series of dams. This was allocated for training barracks for the Leeds Pals. The foundations are still clearly visible, marching up the hill behind the Leeds Pals memorial.

For nine lovely months boys who had lived with cobbles and mill chimneys and market stalls woke every day to curlews and grouse and lapwings. Many of them, in their letters home, spoke of this as being the happiest time of their lives.

A lot of photos survive of the Pals – arriving from Masham station on the little narrow gauge railway, digging trenches and lining up for church parade.

Their faces look out from sepia vignettes, shyly smiling or nervously affecting a steely gaze. They are dressed alike in ill-fitting uniforms, brown belted and brass buttoned.

Inevitably the day came when they marched away and served in Egypt before being slaughtered in France. The few survivors continued to return to Masham and Breary Banks well into the 1970s.
In 2007 Kell Bank School, just down the dale from Breary Banks, made a superb animation that went on to win a number of awards.

The site of the camp at Breary Banks is high on the Dale's side and the views are magnificent. It feels a very happy place.

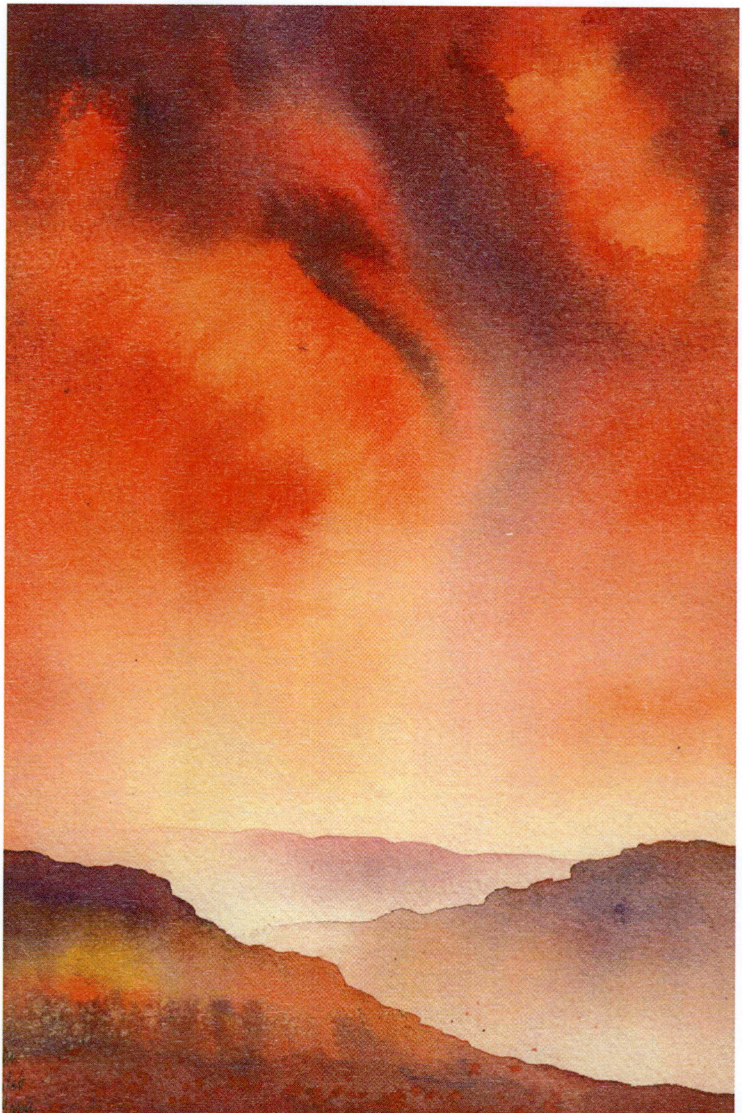

Colsterdale, Evening

The Masham Bones

During the last hundred years or so every time someone dug a hole in or around Masham market place bones would be found. These were sometimes handed to the county archeologist, sometimes arranged on a shelf to gather dust and, in the case of one skull, unearthed when the flagpole footings went in, used as a football.

In 1985 The Bruce Arms was extending its cellar when the builders discovered a quantity of human remains. The pub is in an area known as Dixon Keld (a *keld* is a spring). A few yards away in 1988 work began on new public toilets and, immediately – just below the surface – neat rows of skeletons were revealed. In an archaeological dig lasting six weeks over thirty former residents of Masham came to light.

There had been stories going the rounds for years: the market place was a plague pit, the frequent finding of bones were evidence of William the Conqueror's Wasting of the North, there had been a battle here - but the newly found bones were of people in excellent health who had lived well and had died with none of the gruesome signs of "battle trauma" : they weren't holed by arrows, sliced by swords or hacked by axes.

What had been found was a group of Anglo-Scandinavian people of all ages who had lived between about 670 and 1020. They had been buried in a Christian pattern – laid West to East – and, by their presence, helped to build the case that somewhere nearby had been an early church.

After analysis by Bradford University a small collection of the bones made their last journey to Masham's current churchyard on a beautiful autumn day in 2009 and were laid to rest with a blessing from *The Book of Cerne* – a 9th century prayer book.

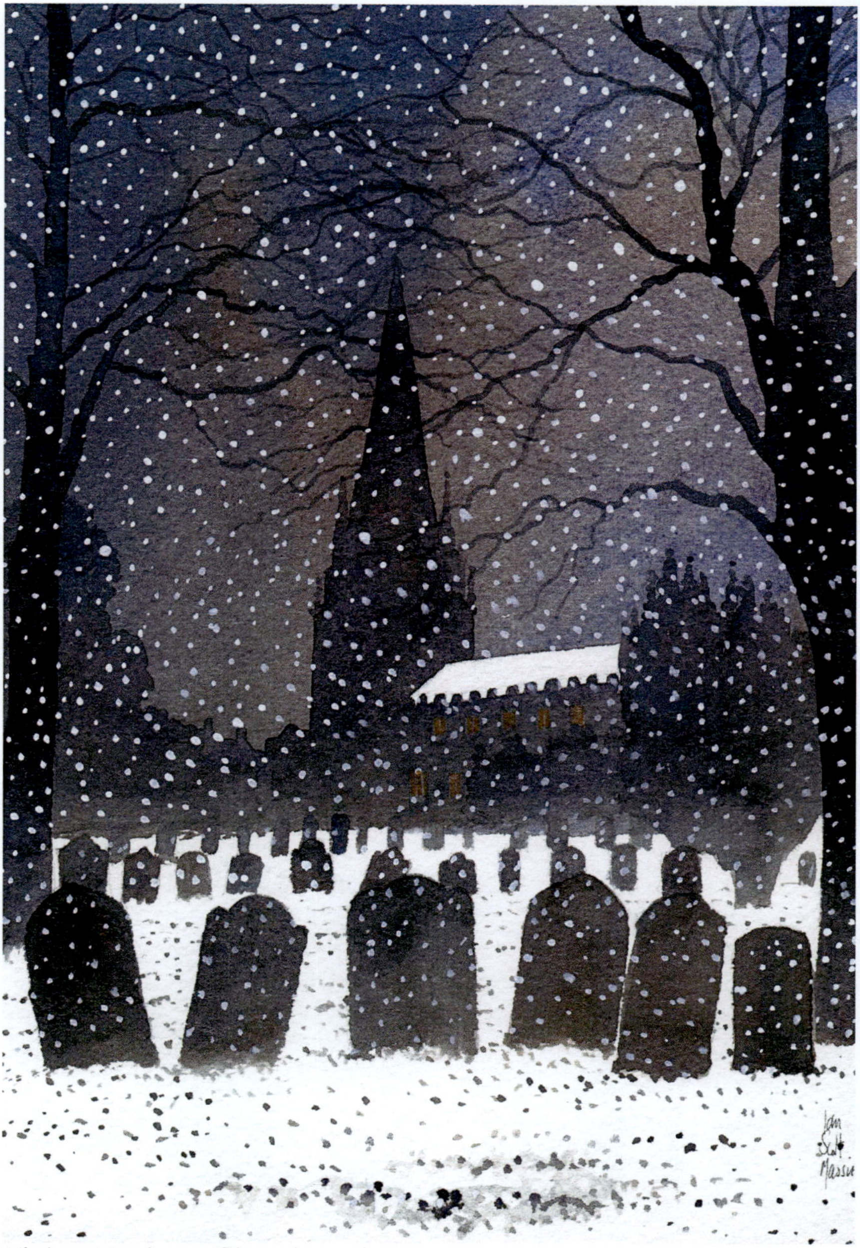

Winter, Masham Churchyard

William Danby & Druid's Temple

William Danby, like most aristocrats of his generation, enjoyed the Grand Tour and, on his return to Swinton Castle, was a man fired with a love all things historical. He made a museum (which is now the bar of Swinton Park hotel) and set about filling it with interesting things. Among the artifacts that came his way were two enormous stone coffins that were found at Marfield near Masham and were originally thought to come from a medieval nunnery. The coffins are now thought to be Roman. William had them installed next to an ornamental pond which he renamed Coffin Lake.

Danby's tenure of Swinton coincided with a mania for grand landscape gardening, folly building and extravagant creations of all kinds by his contemporaries. Danby built a number of interesting additions to Swinton but his tour de force is Druids Temple

What William Danby wanted was the ultimate Neolithic temple. The result has everything - a grotto, guard houses, a sacrificial altar and a huge monolith, latterly named The Phallus. Victorian writers attempted to justify the Temple's construction as a job creation scheme, but, according to local folly expert, Ray Blyth, it was part of Danby's plan "to create a sublimely romantic landscape". As an afterthought Danby advertised for a live-in hermit for a term of seven years and apparently succeeded in finding one. The rigours of living in a stone circle on top of a cold Yorkshire hill for the entertainment of Danby's chums unfortunately proved too much for the poor chap and, after five years he ran away.

Druid's Temple is hard to find – but it's a gem .

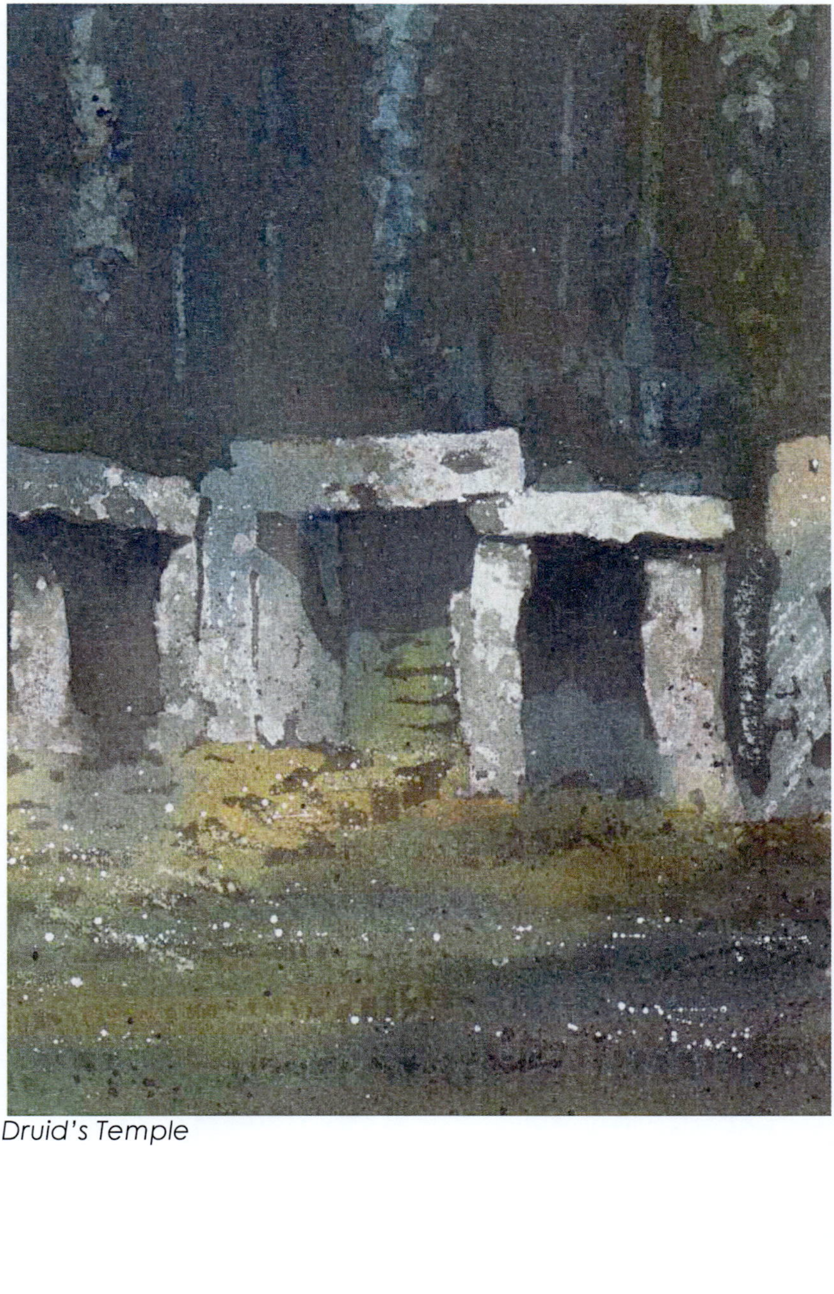

Druid's Temple

Nutwith Cote Stables

Between Masham and Grewelthorpe is a former grange of Fountains Abbey – Nutwith Cote – which has some exceptionally fine stables. The reason for their existence goes back to 1704.

The British Consul in Syria, Thomas Darley, was mad on horses. He found a colt among the Bedouins near Aleppo which made his heart leap. He proposed a deal to Sheik Mizra II, the owner of the colt, and bought the horse for 300 gold sovereigns – a huge amount of money. The Sheik reneged on the deal, however, and so, with a group of sailors, the horse was rustled and smuggled out through Smyrna.

This was to be one of the most successful racehorses of all time. He covered a number of mares, one of which produced the foal known at Bartlett's Childers who sired a string of successful horses at Nutwith Cote. It was for this horse that the beautiful stables were built.

A mile from Nutwith, at Swinton Castle, lived the splendidly named Octavious Harcourt. He owned a very successful horse – Ellington – who won the Epsom Derby and the Doncaster Champagne stakes in 1855 and 56. Put out to stud he sired the amazing Flying Dutchman who won fourteen out of his fifteen races.

St. Paul's church, Healey, near Swinton, was supposedly built with money entirely gained from Ellington's career.

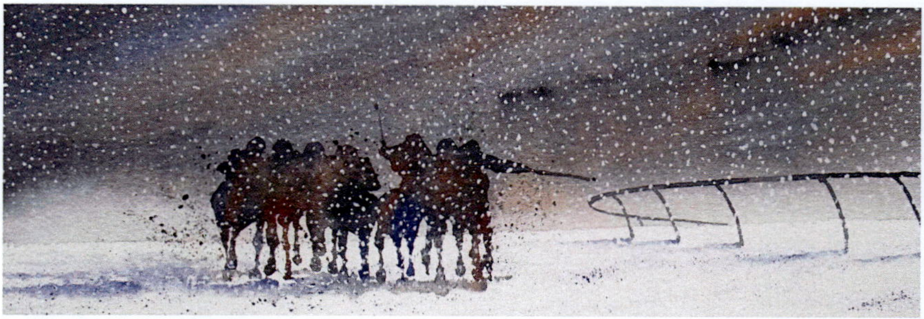

Riders in the Snow

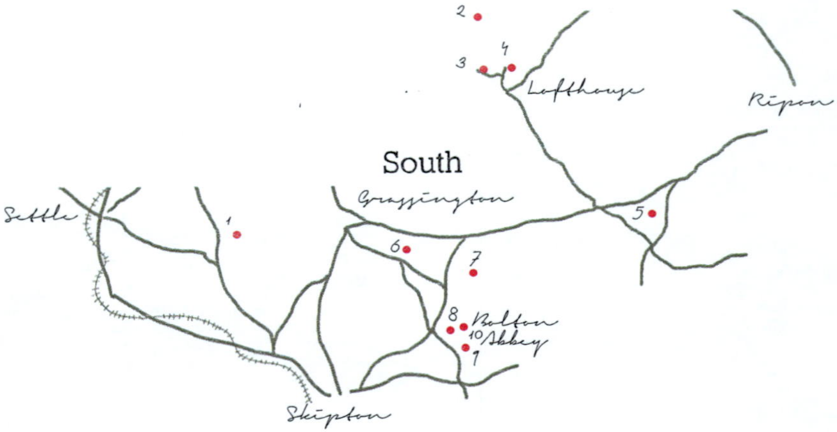

1 Janet's Foss
2 Dead Man's Hill
3 Highwayman of How Stean Gorge
4 St Chad
5 Brimham Rocks
6 Elbolton Hill
7 Troller's Gill
8 The Shepherd Lord
9 The Little Dog Laughed
10 The Strid

Janet's Foss

Behind the lovely waterfall of Janet's Foss is a cave, hidden by the falling water. This is the home of Janet – Queen of the Fairies. Her name lacks the grandeur of Titania but her Foss[1] is beautiful. There's another cave close by called Janet's Cave which visitors often mistake for the fairy's home but this was just an unmagical overnight shelter for travelers and itinerant workers in past times.

The pool below the falls was used as a sheep wash, the water thought to bless the sheep with good health. Charles Kingsley knew this place and its stories, and he drew inspiration for *The Water Babies* from here, Malham Tarn and Arncliffe .

It's a gorgeous spot but has been a bit of a focus for deranged fairy hunters. Viscount Torrington, a Georgian traveler and diarist, was one of these. He turned out a dreadful little poem after a visit here:

Little Gennet, Fairy trim,
To the merry Dance leads on
Full of pastime, full of whim,
With her playmate, Oberon.

.

Enough said....

[1]Foss is an Old Norse word for a waterfall. It pops up in slightly altered form at High Force and a few other places.

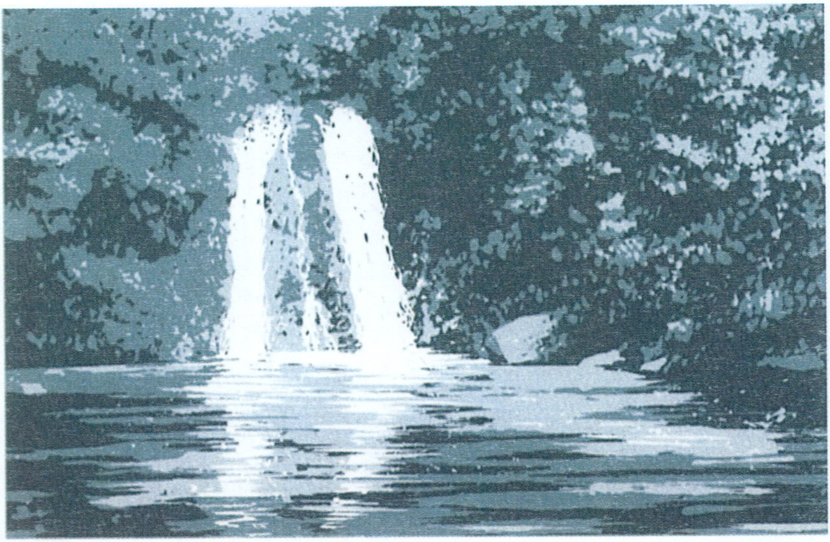

Janet's Foss

Dead Man's Hill

This is a story which has a lots of storytellers' fingerprints on so I'm going to tell the version I heard first, which I think is the best.

Three drovers and a dog came down from Scotland with a herd of cattle bound for Bradford market. They were hoping to sell some Highland cattle that had been seized by the English in the hard years after the battle of Culloden.

At Lodge, on the slopes of what would soon be known as Dead Man's Hill, they stayed within an inn kept by a woman and her daughter.

A few days later they returned with the price of the cattle in their pockets and stayed the night. Unfortunately this time they stayed more than the night.

After getting the drovers drunk the two women murdered the men as they slept. They cut off their heads and buried the bodies and heads in two different places on the hill. They had reckoned without the dog, however.

No matter how they tried they couldn't catch or scare away the faithful sheepdog. Of course, sooner or later some travellers making for Lodge saw the dog digging and went to have a closer look. Out of the ground came one head, then a second and then a third.

There are two versions of the endgame:

In the first the two women were taken to Pateley Bridge, tried and hung.

In the second the two were found to be witches and were mysteriously petrified. They stand as two weathered stones, known as Jenny Twig and her Daughter Tib, overlooking Nidderdale near Lofthouse.

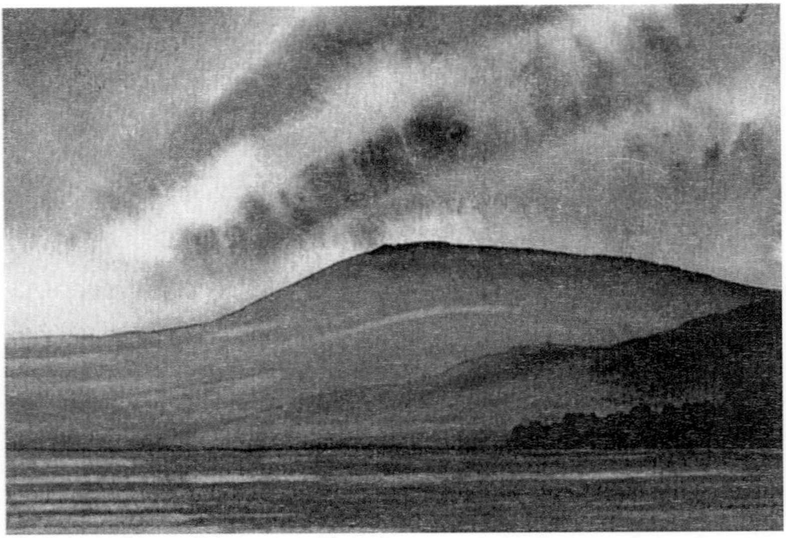

Dead Man's Hill

The Highwayman of How Stean Gorge

How Steam Gorge in Upper Nidderdale is an amazing testament to the eroding power of water. The deep gorge is extremely impressive, and there is a cave here with a story.

Tom Taylor's Cave takes its name from a highwayman who used this as his hideout. It's quite a way from the nearest highway but, I suppose, with a decent horse, perhaps the commute wasn't too arduous.

There seemed to be no evidence for this tale until a pile of gold and silver coins turned up. However, when these were examined they were found to be Roman. Could it be that a legend of buried treasure (maybe helped along by the occasional appearance of a coin) gradually mutated over time to the story of a highwayman and his ill-gotten gains?

It's worth a trip to make up your mind. How Stean Gorge, like Ibbeth Peril in Dentdale, is a great surprise. Until you look down into it you have no idea, from the lie of the surrounding countryside, that its there.

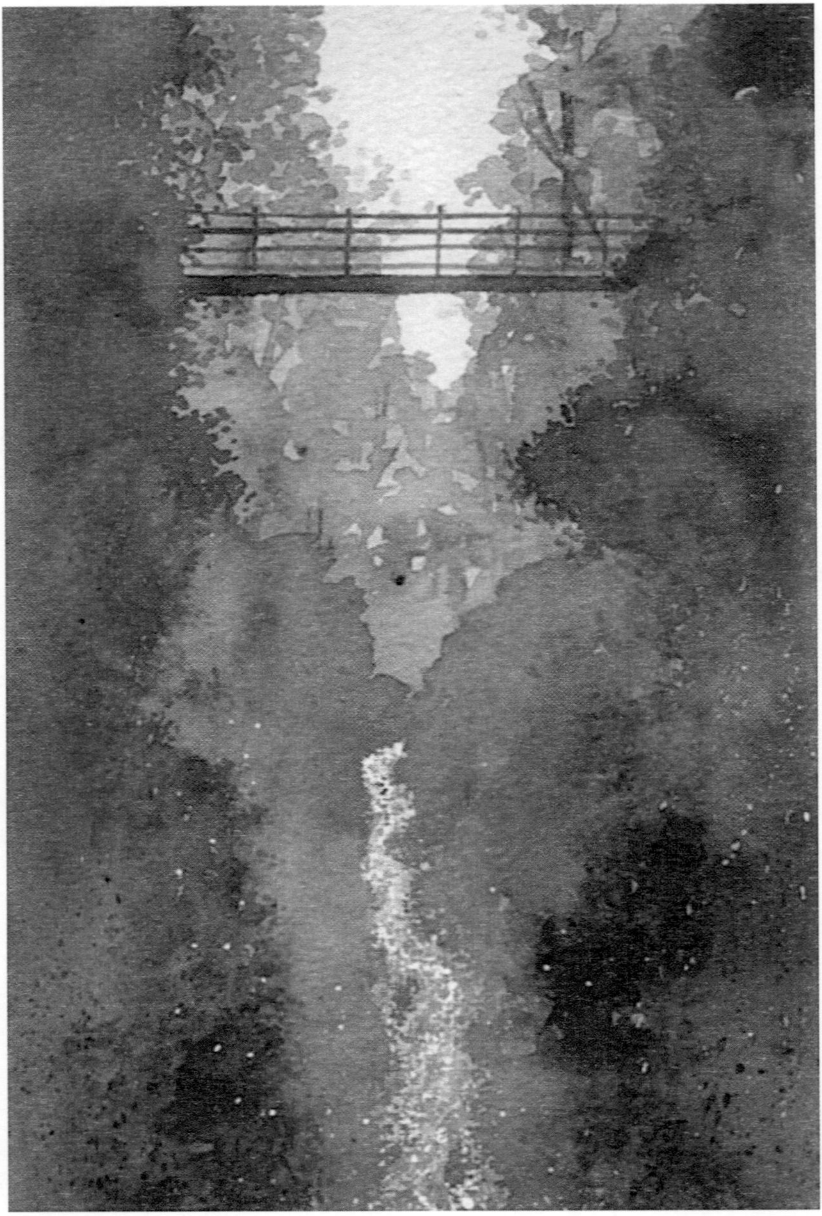

How Stean Gorge

St Chad 's Church, Middlesmoor

St. Chad was a pupil of St. Aidan at Lindisfarne. He studied with Bede and fought the case for the Celtic church (which was eventually suppressed in favour of the church of Rome) at the royal court in Wessex. Toward the end of his life he travelled across the North of England from Lastingham, where he was abbot, setting up little centres for prayer and worship. He liked to travel on foot, which an Archbishop of Canterbury once insisted was undignified, and bodily put Chad onto a horse.

In a field, on a hill, at the head of Nidderdale he found a place that he considered a place of angels. With a valley to each side and a view across the heights of Northumbria he had a stone cross set up on which, after his death, someone carved CROS CEADDA – Chad's cross. So, at Middlesmoor, the flame of the Christian word was kept alight through the Dark Ages.

His death, when it came a couple of years later in 572, was the stuff of legend. A monk who heard the sound of angelic voices coming from the oratory at Lichfield Minster, went to Chad and asked what this meant. Chad told him, after asking the monk to keep his words secret, that the angels had come to tell Chad he would be called to his heavenly reward in seven days. A week passed, Chad became frail, and died on 2nd March, which is his saint's day.

And now, in the tiny church in the place of angels, pilgrims of all persuasions unwrap their sandwiches and look out at the Northumbrian rain and praise all manner of saints – Wainwright, Cadbury, Theakston, the Ordnance Survey, and perhaps the man himself – in the shadow of Chad's Cross.

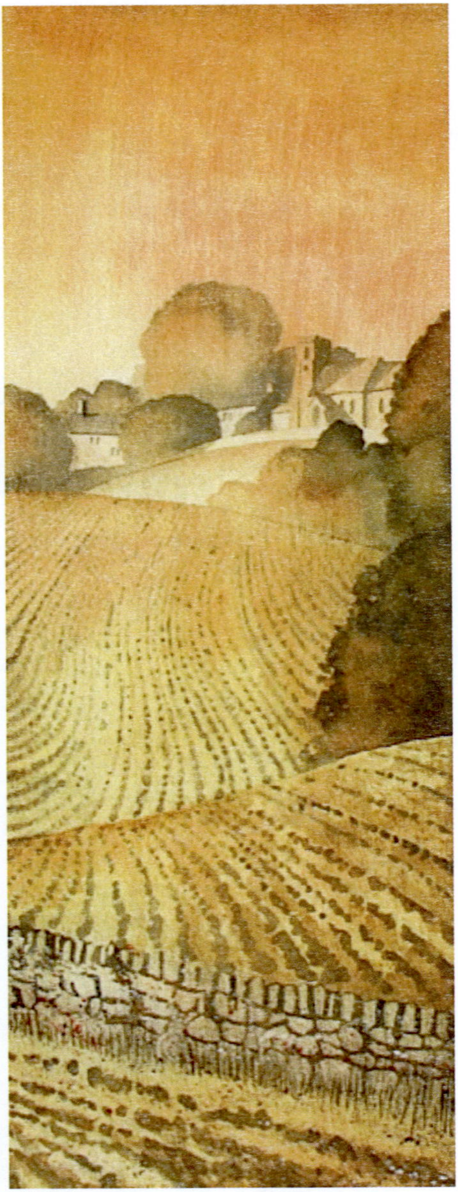

Middlesmoor

Brimham Rocks

There was once, over three hundred million years ago, a huge river which drained much of Norway and Scotland. The water carried eroded minerals from the Norwegian granite mountains and formed an enormous delta, half the size of Yorkshire. Layer upon layer built up: crystals of feldspar and quartz mingled with grit and sand which formed Millstone Grit – the hard stone which caps many of Yorkshire's hills. Ripples and dunes formed in the rock and the layers built up at an angle towards the movement of the water. Millions of years passed in which glaciers, rain and wind, freezing and thawing by turns, shaped Brimham Rocks into strange, animal like forms, the soft layers often undercutting the harder layers above.

The rocks are very beautiful and, on a fine day, one of the loveliest places in Yorkshire. In autumn the bilberry bushes are laden with purple fruit, grouse clatter and bark out of the heather and the views stretch away to distant horizons in every direction. As for the rocks themselves most have acquired names – the Dancing Bear, the Eagle, the Writing Desk – and some have acquired stories. Here are two of the best known.

A guidebook of 1863 tells the story of Edwin and Julia. Edwin lived in a village near the rocks and Julia was the daughter of a wealthy landowner. Edwin asked Julia's father for her hand in marriage and was, in the best traditions of this kind of story, turned down flat. Furthermore, the enraged father refused to let the lovers see each other again.

They made a suicide pact and vowed to throw themselves from a precipice at Brimham. Julia's father, however, discovered his daughter's farewell letter and, distraught and terrified, rode his horse to the rocks to try to prevent the tragedy. Mistaking his intentions, the lovers leapt as he approached but, miraculously, were borne up by a strong wind and landed safely again on the cliff edge.

Whether it was the fairies which dwell in the rocks, the legendary druids of Brimham or Julia's excessively voluminous dress that saved the day is immaterial. Her father consented to their marriage and they lived happily ever after.

There is a rock at Brimham which has a narrow space hollowed out within it and a narrow tunnel sixteen feet long which has been worn by erosion to the rock's exterior. This is the Oracle or Great Cannon. A 1781 paper from the Society of Antiquaries describes at length this remarkable stone and how it may have been used:

"In the abovementioned aperture, a man might lay concealed, and predict future events to those that came to consult the oracle, and is heard distinctly on the north side of the rock where the hole is not visible. This might make the credulous Britons think the predictions proceeded solely from the rock deity."

The writer goes on to say that this – and other stones with holes in – proves that the Druids of the Ancient Britons had a culture of rock deities from which they discerned the future. It seems that scientific rigour has moved on since 1781.

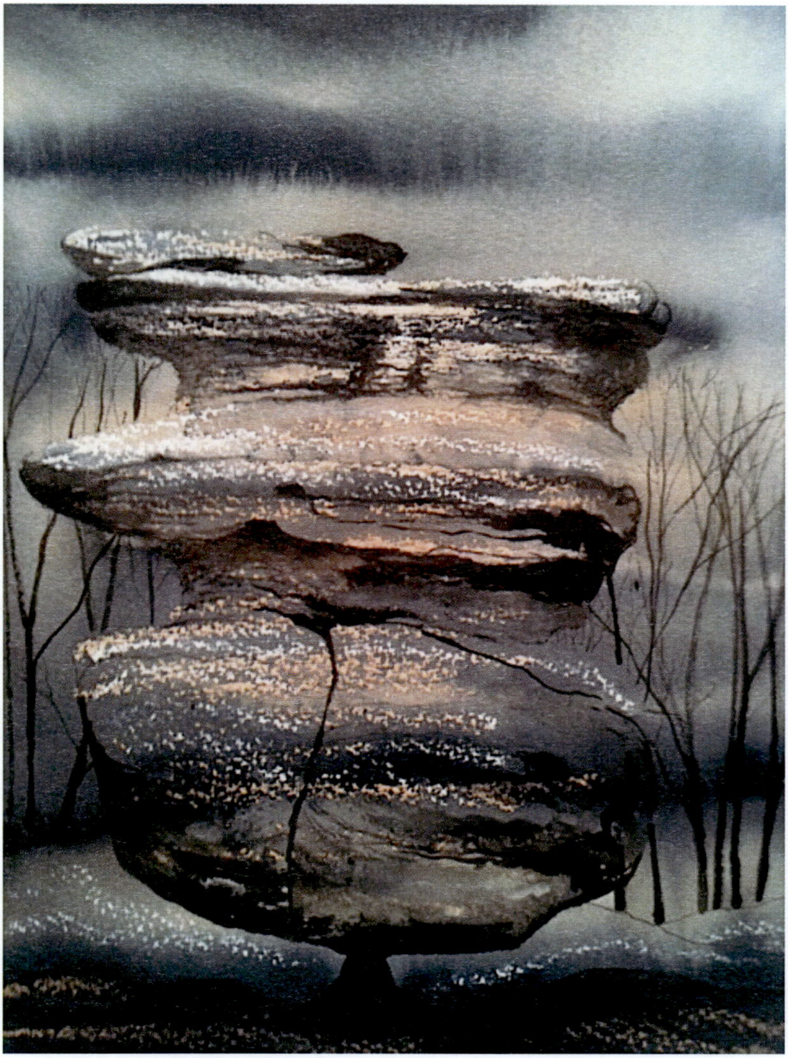

The Balancing Rock, Brimham Rocks

Elbolton Hill

The hill of the fairies overlooks Thorpe, near Burnsall. It has a distinctive shape and a host of stories are clustered about it.

Navvy Noddle hole, for example, a cave on the Eastern slopes of the hill, is reputed to be the haunt of fairies. In 1888, the cave was excavated and found to contain the bones of recent and extinct creatures, but, unfortunately, no fairy bones. The strangest discovery was that of a group of twelve men seated around the remains of a long-cold fire. Had all twelve died simultaneously? The mystery remains unsolved.

What is known for certain is that the fairies were seen here as recently as the nineteenth century.

A man was walking home from Burnsall on a fine moonlit night. On the path ahead of him he saw a great company of fairies, each taking turns to sing and dance. They were feather light, dressed in green, and their diaphanous wings shimmered in the light of the moon.

He was delighted – the stories were true after all - and he quietly watched the show from the shadows of a tree. However, he was a man who liked a song and, so, forgetting himself after a while, felt compelled to join in. Of course part of him knew instinctively that this kind of intrusion always infuriates fairies.

Not surprisingly, they were incensed at his rudeness and unimpressed by his amateur rendering of the music hall ballad he had chosen as his party piece. They gave him a pretty good thumping.

He turned and ran but, on an ill-advised impulse, snatched up a sample fairy to show his children and to corroborate his story. He knew only too well that they would think he had simply been on the beer, as usual.

Arriving home he could feel the furious fairy in his buttoned down pocket but, having told his children to expect the surprise of their lives, opened his pocket to find it empty. He went to bed a disappointed man. As his children's derisory laughter was ringing in his ears, he could swear it was echoed by some decidedly ethereal giggling in the moonlight outside the window.

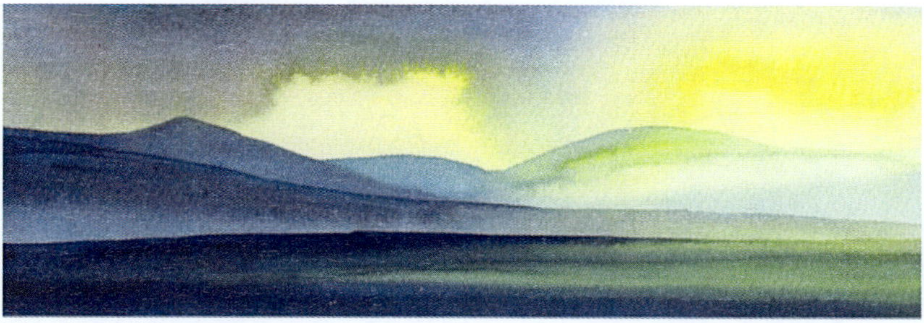

Elbolton Hill

Troller's Gill

There is an innocent looking track that meanders beside the stream at Skyreholme. Yellow wagtails dip above the brown water and bob on the rocks. Lapwings tumble above the alders. Across the stream, through the tress, the gardens of Parcevall Hall adorn the slopes.

The track becomes more defined. Here and there are grass-grown stone embankments, shallow cuttings between shaggy bracken hills and a sense that beneath one's feet is a very old road.

A strange landscape unfolds to reveal a cleft in a wall of stone and turf. Its scale is hard to appreciate until, standing at the entrance to the impressive gorge, the walls tower overhead.

The atmosphere seems darkly oppressive. The ravine is narrow and huge boulders lie scattered before the walker's feet. Ahead, the floor of the gorge rises, curving out of sight, into the shadows of Troller's Gill. There are several stories about this place and, when you stand here, it is remarkably easy to believe them.

A ghostly dog – a barguest or padfoot – lives here with "eyes as big as saucers", eyes which flame, burn and will kill you if you look into them. Arthur Conan Doyle's mother lived not far from Ingleton and would have known this story so it is possibly connected in direct descent to the Hound of the Baskervilles.

There is a story that a man who lived near the Gill, and who had laughed at the stories, decided to spend the night at Troller's Gill. He walked into the ravine, on a dark night of howling gales, and made for an old yew tree in the heart of the Gill. He had come prepared with a charm to protect him. He therefore drew a circle on the ground, spoke the spell and knelt to kiss the ground three times.

Confident that he was well protected he summoned the beast by calling out and, out of the darkness the shaggy shape of the enormous dog appeared, its huge eyes glowing red in the night.

His body, or what scattered pieces remained of it, was found by a shepherd the following morning. The charm, it seemed, had no effect on the beast and the barguest remains a fearful presence to this day.

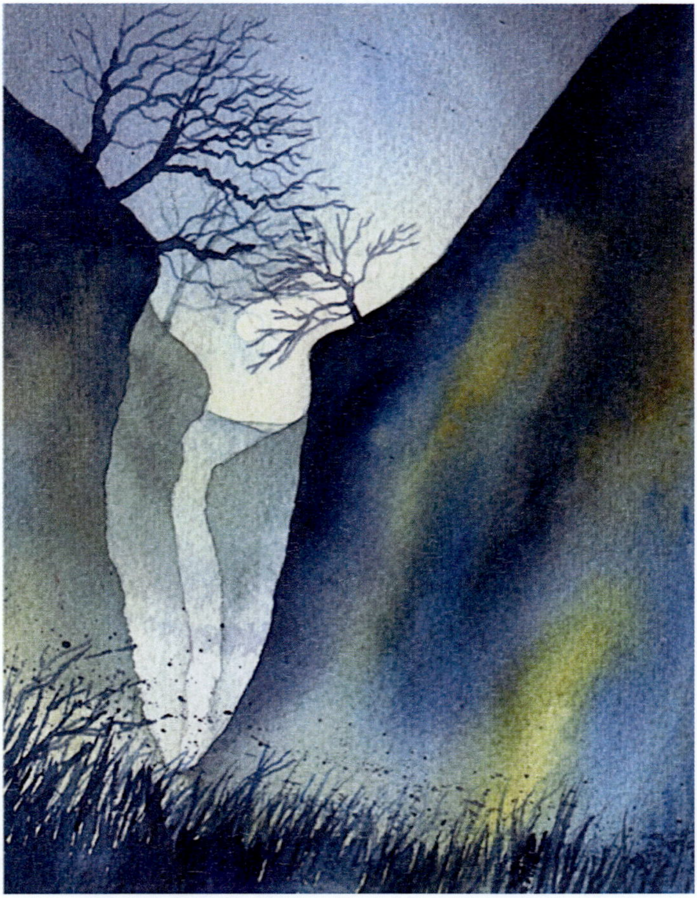

Troller's Gill

The Shepherd Lord

The Wars of the Roses were, like most medieval conflicts, a struggle for power and wealth between a few titled individuals. Most of the fighting and dying – of which there was little shortage – was to be the role of the peasantry, while the lords and knights, wrapped in their protective tin cans on enormous shire horses, usually lived to fight another day.

For the young Edmund, Duke of Rutland, however, this was not to be. After the Battle of Wakefield in which the House of Lancaster was triumphant, Rutland was stripped on his arms and armour, a defenceless, wounded prisoner. The action had resulted in the deaths of Edmund's father and brother-in-law and he fully expected to be ransomed, as was the accepted process of the time.

His captor, Sir John Clifford – Baron of Skipton Castle, High Sherriff of Westmorland – was about to earn his nickname of 'Butcher'. Having found out his prisoner's identity, Clifford drew a dagger and buried it to the hilt in the boy's heart. (Clifford died a few months later as he removed his helmet to take a drink of water, and was struck in the throat by a well named arrow.)

Clifford's wife feared for her children's lives when, as she dreaded, the Yorkists were finally triumphant. She sent the young heir to live with a shepherd's family at Threkeld near Keswick and so, until his thirty-second year, the inheritor of one of England's richest dynasties lived in a thatched, moorland cottage in ignorance of his identity. He could not read and only ever learned to write his name.

In time the political landscape changed and he came into his own. However he rejected the baronial splendour of Skipton Castle and chose to live at the lovely Barden tower. His greatest pleasure was stargazing from Barden's roof.

He cemented his family's reputation with the Tudor court late in life when, aged 60, he led the troops of Craven against the Scots at Flodden. His story lends to Barden Tower just the right element of romance to the perfect romantic ruin.

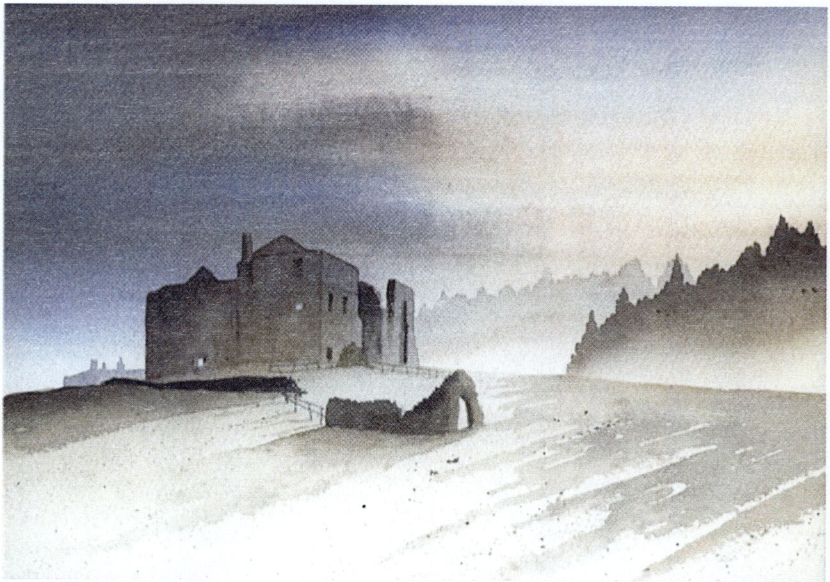

Barden Tower

The Little Dog Laughed

There are a pair of laughing dogs carved in stone at Bolton Abbey, and from these petrified canines has come a tumbling outpouring of stories which link them to:

Hey diddle diddle, the cat and the fiddle,
The cow jumped over the moon.
The little dog laughed to see such fun
And the dish ran away with the spoon.

Most of these stories are born out of the happy coincidence of some names: a prior of Bolton Abbey called Richard Moone, the Hey family (cattle farmers apparently who profited from the dissolution of the abbey) and a Latin translation of the words for Catholic faith.

Out of the many and bizarre interpretations I am indebted to the Long Preston History Group for having put together the most lucid explanation and here it is, with one or two useful additions from other sources:

"*Hey diddle diddle the cat and the fiddle*"

A farming family – the Heys – had turned protestant, just prior to the Reformation and had left the Catholic faith (in Latin: Catholica Fide). The head of the family had traded cattle with Richard Moone – the last Prior of Bolton – and swindled him. Hey also profited by the dissolution of the abbey.

"*The cow jumped over the moon*"

"*The little dog laughed to see such fun*"

There are two carved, laughing dogs on the tower of Bolton Priory (there may be a third, or it could just be a baboon with structural problems).

"And the dish ran away with the spoon"

The daughter of the cattle farmer was to be wed but could only do so in her parish church – at Bolton Priory –for which Moone refused permission. She –the dish – therefore eloped (ran away) with her beloved – the spoon.

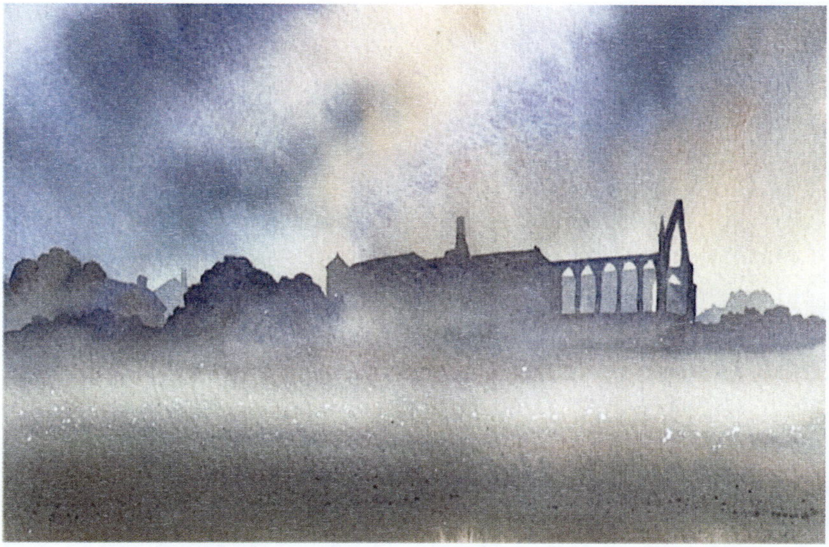

Bolton Abbey

The Strid

The Strid is one of the strangest places in England. Yorkshire is a county rich with examples of what water can do - complex cave systems many miles long with caverns the size of cathedrals, rivers that disappear and reappear, incredibly beautiful waterfalls - but the Strid is simply remarkable for its seeming innocence and its deadly character.

The River Wharfe, a little way upstream, is a broad, substantial river but it narrows to less than a couple of metres at the Strid. Effectively the river is standing on its side – that breadth has become depth – and beneath the flat rocks of the Strid is a deep, dark channel.

No one knows how deep the river is here – the many currents and complex, unseen caverns confound any attempts at measurement. But this is a very famous place for a very chilling reason. It has a one hundred per cent mortality rate: no one has fallen or jumped into the Strid and lived. In most cases the corpses are never found. Their remains are presumably pinned by the current to the walls of underwater formations until they disintegrate and disappear.

The death toll is a long one stretching back centuries and tragically, has recently been added to by a honeymoon couple in 1998 and an eight year-old boy in 2010.

The most famous story attached to this dreadful place is that of the young Lord Egremont.

Egremont was in Strid Woods with his greyhounds and huntsman. Among the dogs was a bitch and Egremont was holding her leash. At the bitch's heels was her pup. Coming to the rocks at the water's edge Egremont paused to judge the distance of the stream. And then, deaf to the warning cries of the huntsman, leapt across the narrow gap but, just as his feet touched the far rock he felt an insistent tug at the leash in his hand. Unwilling to risk the life of her pup, his greyhound was pulling him irrevocably backwards. With a startled cry, and a horrid realisation, he tumbled backwards and was lost forever in the swirling water,

In tears the huntsman brought the awful news of the boy's death to his mother. After days of dark mourning had passed, Lady Alice de Romilly, heartbroken, and now with no heir to her fortune, gave the land that she owned to Bolton Priory with the words: "Many a poor man shall be my heir".

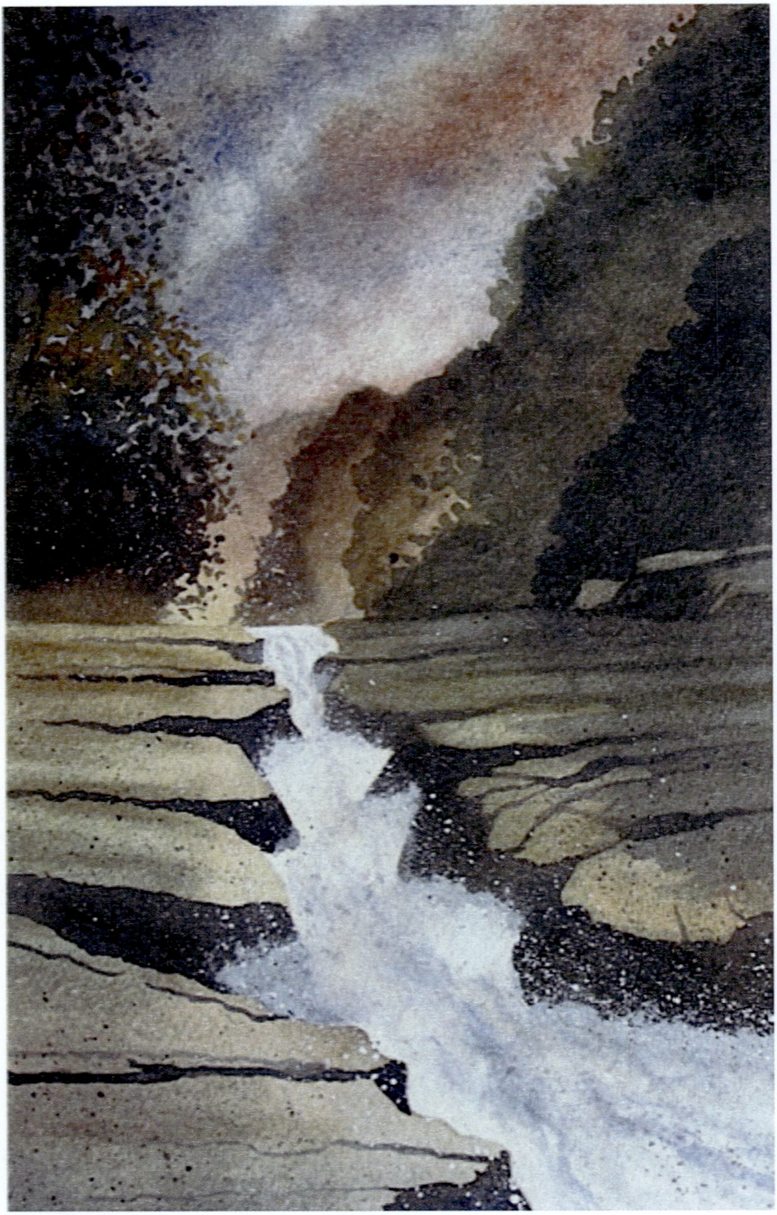

The Strid

Ackowledgements

The information for these stories came from many sources. I am deeply indebted to Ian Johnson, Kirsten Antoncich, Jackie Masterman, Shane Metcalfe, Ray Blyth, Susan Briggs, Penny Seckerson (who looks after Wensley church), Graham White and Dawn Lancaster of the Churches Conservation Trust, Charlotte Morrison, Ken Jackson, Elaine Falshaw and many others who, over the years, have shared their knowledge of the history and folklore of the Yorkshire Dales with me or helped me organise the exhibition The Tales of The Dales. As always my greatest thanks go to my wife, Josie Beszant, who has helped me enormously through the biggest project I have undertaken to date.

I've listed some useful sources below - this is just a small selection.

Useful books about the Dales and beyond:
Out of all these sources the writings of W R Mitchell (for a long time editor of *The Dalesman)* and Arthur Raistrick (who wrote the definitive *The Pennine Dales*) are particularly worth seeking out.

Susan Cunliffe-Lister: *Days of Yore* (Wilton 65, 1978)
Mike Harding & Tom Stephenson: *Walking The Dales* (Michael Joseph, 1987)
Marie Hartley & Joan Ingleby: *Life & Tradition in the Yorkshire Dales* (Dent, 1968)
James Herriot: *James Herriot's Yorkshire* (Michael Joseph, 1979)
W R Mitchell: *High Dale Country* (Souvenir Press, 1991)
Howard Peach: *Curious Tales of Old North Yorkshire* (Sigma Leisure 2004)
Arthur Raistrick: *The Pennine Dales* (Eyre Methuen, 1968)
Reader's Digest: *Folklore, Myths & Legends of Britain* (RD, 1977)
Roland Smith: *On Foot In The Yorkshire Dales* (David & Charles, 1996)
Summer Strevens: *Haunted Yorkshire Dales* (The History Press, 2011)

Yorkshire Dales Nat Park: *Ancient Trackways* (YDNPA, 2006)

Websites:

Out of Oblivion: A Landscape Through Time is a great site created by the Yorkshire Dales Park Authority. There is a wealth of detailed information on here. There are thousands of websites offering information on Dales stories and legends. This is just a few that are particularly interesting.

Fabulous Follies	www.fabulousfollies.net
Haunted Yorkshire Dales	www.hauntedyorkshiredales.co.uk
Out of Oblivion:	www.outofoblivion.or.uk
The Tate Gallery:	www.tate.org.uk
(includes Turner's drawings of many Dales locations)	
The Megalithic Portal:	www.megalithic.co.uk

About the Pictures

The paintings and prints for this book and the accompanying exhibition were mostly painted over a two year period. The media used include watercolour, Indian ink and screen print. As the work progressed I found that I developed a palette for the Dales (which excluded a couple of my usual favourite pigments) as I moved towards a way to capture the personality of the landscape I was walking through. The colours which formed this palette were: burnt sienna, quinacridone gold, ultramarine blue, Winsor blue, permanent rose, alizarin crimson, new gamboge, indigo and neutral tint.

Most of the pictures started life as pencil sketches through which I explored the shapes and the fall of light which give the Dales their wonderful character. These sketches sometimes began on the tops of hills in the pouring rain, sometimes laid on the warm grass of a summer meadow and sometimes shivering with cold in a snowy lane. The weather, as I have known for a long time, is an essential ingredient in capturing the magic of the Dales.